TRANSFORMATIONAL
LEADERSHIP
UNLEASHING YOUR FULL POTENTIAL
A COACHING GUIDE

I0555310

DR. JONATHAN K. JEFFERSON

Written By: Dr. Jonathan K. Jefferson
Edited By: Dr. Harvey Fields
Cover and Interior Design: Aaron C. Butler

ISBN: 9781967082773 (Paperback)
ISBN: 9781967082780 (eBook)
Library of Congress Control Number: 2025923500

© 2025 Dr. Jonathan K. Jefferson

All rights reserved. This book or any portion thereof may not be reproduced in any form without permission from the copyright holder, except as permitted by U.S. Copyright law.
Printed in the United States of America

BookButler Publishing Company
Upper Marlboro, MD 20774
TheBookButler.com

BookButler Publishing Company titles may be purchased in bulk for educational, business, fundraising, or sales promotional use. For information, please email: info@thebookbutler.com

Preface / Introduction – How to Use This Book

Leadership is both art and practice. This book is designed as a **coaching companion**—a resource you can study, apply, and return to as your leadership journey evolves. Each chapter blends insight with action, moving you from awareness to application.

Every chapter follows a consistent rhythm:

1. **Concepts and Frameworks** – Foundational ideas that define each leadership theme.

2. **Case Study** – A short scenario showing how the principle works in practice.

3. **Conclusion** – Key insights that summarize the chapter's lessons.

4. **Next Steps** – Practical actions you can take immediately to strengthen your leadership.

5. **Reflection and Worksheet** – Space to process what you've learned, apply it to your context, and plan your next move.

Use this book at your own pace. Some leaders work through a chapter each week; others focus on one section at a time and integrate the exercises into coaching sessions or team meetings.

Whichever approach you choose, the goal is progress—not perfection. Leadership transformation happens through **consistent reflection, small experiments, and courageous conversations.**

You will get the most from this book if you:

- Read with curiosity rather than judgment.

- Pause at the reflection prompts and write down honest answers.

- Share what you're learning with a colleague or mentor.

Whether you lead a classroom, a business, a ministry, or your own household, these pages are meant to guide you in **living and leading on purpose.**

For readers who want to put these principles into daily practice, a companion volume — **Transformational Leadership Workbook: Your Coaching Companion to Unleashing Your Full Potential** *— provides guided exercises, reflection pages, and action tools aligned with each chapter.*

TRANSFORMATIONAL LEADERSHIP
WORKBOOK
YOUR COACHING COMPANION TO UNLEASHING YOUR FULL POTENTIAL

DR. JONATHAN K. JEFFERSON

Table of Contents

The Hidden Weight Leaders Carry

Every leader faces a kind of personal *kryptonite*—the invisible drain that weakens clarity, confidence, or conviction. It can appear as burnout, procrastination, fear of failure, over-commitment, or the quiet sense that you're leading on autopilot. Left unchecked, this "KRYPTONITE Syndrome" erodes effectiveness from the inside out.

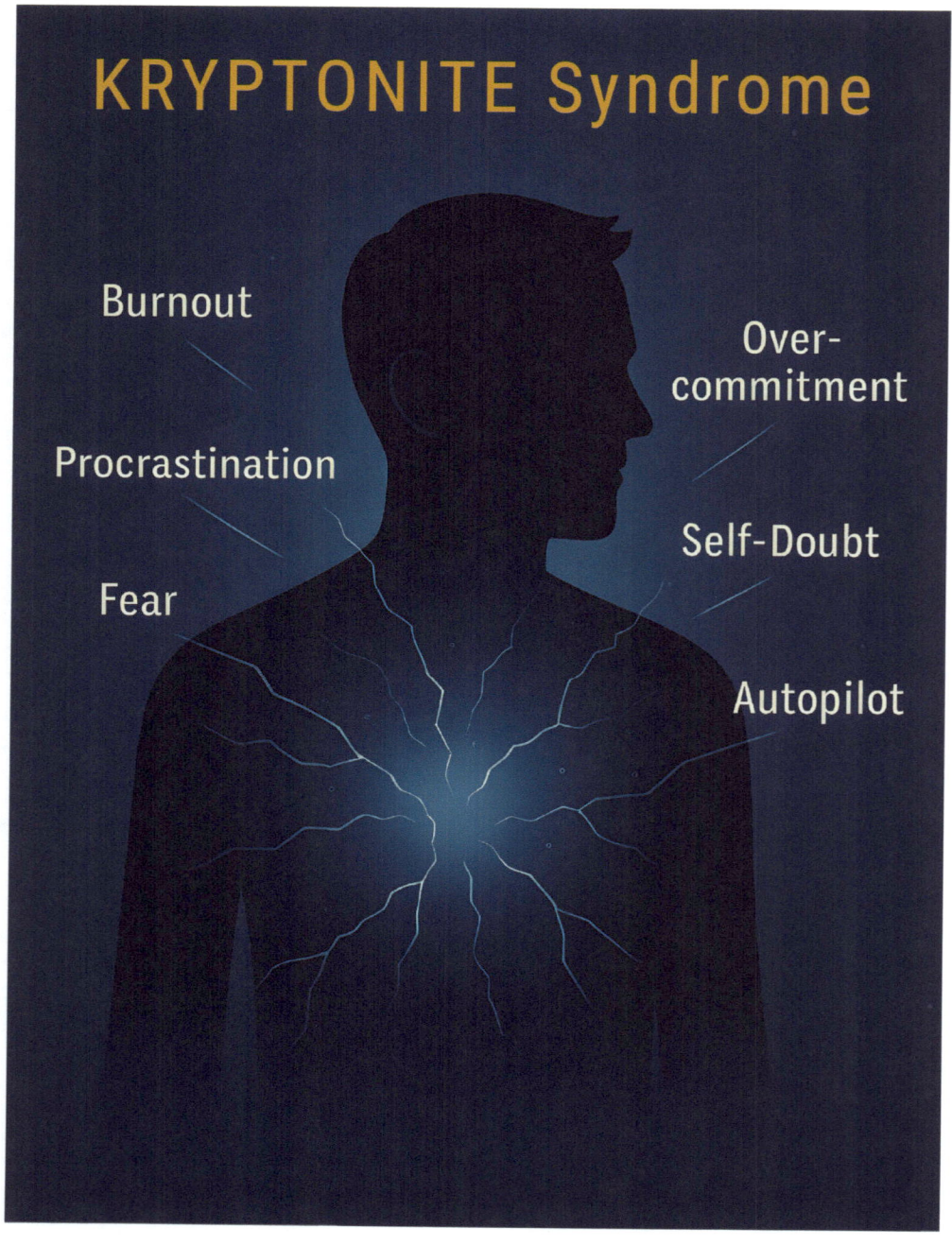

Naming the Problem

KRYPTONITE Syndrome isn't about a lack of skill; it's about misalignment. When your values, energy, and actions fall out of sync, even small tasks feel heavy. The purpose of this book is to help you recognize where your leadership power leaks away—and show you how to reclaim it.

The Antidote: Transformation from Within

Transformational leadership begins by re-energizing the leader. Through coaching, reflection, and intentional growth, you rebuild self-awareness and realign purpose with practice. The chapters ahead will guide you through that process, teaching you how to:

- Reconnect with your core values.

- Lead with authenticity and empathy.

- Build teams that thrive on trust and vision.

- Navigate change with clarity and resilience.

Leading Life Before Leading Others

Transformational leadership begins long before you step into a meeting, build a team, or launch a new initiative. It begins with how you lead yourself. A leader who lives without clarity of purpose may still achieve short-term success, but true influence—lasting, life-giving influence—flows from personal alignment.

Living on purpose means designing your life with intention rather than reaction. It's about ensuring that the energy you bring to leadership is sustained by the life you live outside of it. Before you can effectively lead others, you must lead yourself toward wholeness.

The *Living Life on Purpose* framework identifies **eight areas of life** that together form the foundation for balance and fulfillment:

1. **Health** – Caring for your physical and emotional well-being so that energy and vitality support your mission.

2. **Financial** – Managing resources wisely to build freedom, stability, and integrity.

3. **Social** – Nurturing meaningful relationships and connections that strengthen community and collaboration.

4. **Intellectual** – Pursuing continuous learning, curiosity, and creative thought to stay adaptable and innovative.

5. **Spiritual** – Grounding yourself in faith, values, and inner peace that guide your decisions and restore perspective.

6. **Family** – Building strong bonds and shared values that anchor you beyond professional achievement.

7. **Career** – Aligning your work with your purpose so that your profession becomes an expression of who you are, not just what you do.

8. **Other (Legacy/Service)** – Contributing to something greater than yourself through giving, mentoring, or community impact.

These areas work together like spokes on a wheel. When one spoke is weak or neglected, the ride becomes uneven. When all are aligned, you move forward smoothly and with purpose.

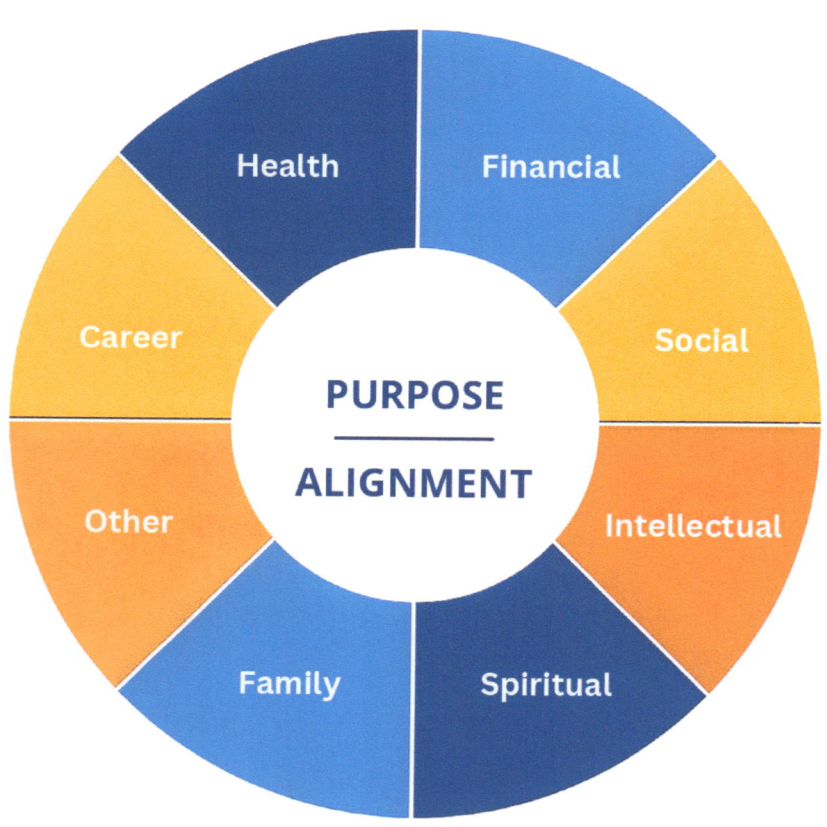

On-Purpose Pause:

Which of these life areas feels most aligned with your purpose right now? Which one needs more attention or realignment?

Transformational leaders don't separate personal and professional purpose—they integrate them. Your influence grows not from the title you hold but from the wholeness you cultivate. By strengthening each area of your life, you create a foundation that allows your leadership to be steady, authentic, and deeply human.

Why It Matters

When you neutralize your own kryptonite—those habits, fears, or mindsets that drain your strength—you unlock the capacity to transform others. Energized, focused leaders create energized, focused organizations.

How This Book Can Help

Each chapter offers frameworks, examples, and tools to help you identify barriers, take purposeful action, and build habits that sustain growth. Think of this not as a manual to read once, but as a **coaching journey** you can revisit whenever your energy or direction wavers.

Kryptonite   Awareness   Realignment Transformation

So before you turn the page, pause for one reflection:

What is your kryptonite right now—what quietly drains your leadership strength?

Write it down. You'll return to that answer throughout this book as you learn to replace exhaustion with empowerment, confusion with clarity, and stagnation with sustainable progress.

Reflection: Identifying Your Leadership Kryptonite

Take a few quiet minutes before moving into Chapter 1 to reflect honestly on where your leadership energy is being drained. These prompts are designed to surface both internal and external kryptonite sources—so you can start this journey with clarity.

1. **Energy Check** – When do you feel most energized in your leadership? When do you feel most depleted?

2. **Alignment Audit** – Which of your daily responsibilities reflect your core values—and which don't?

3. **Hidden Kryptonite** – What recurring thoughts, habits, or fears quietly undermine your confidence or focus?

4. **Support Network** – Who helps you regain perspective when you feel stuck or overwhelmed?

5. **Commitment to Change** – What's one small shift you can make this week to begin restoring your leadership energy?

Remember: awareness precedes change. You cannot transform what you haven't named.

Reflective Practice
Identifying Your Leadership Kryptonite

Take a few quiet minutes before moving into Chapter 1 to reflect honestly on where your leadership energy is being drained. These prompts are designed to surface both internal and external kryptonite sources—so you can start this journey with clarity.

Energy Check – When do you feel most energized in your leadership? When do you feel most depleted?

Alignment Audit – Which of your daily responsibilities reflect your core values and which don't?

Hidden Kryptonite – What recurring thoughts, habits, or fears quietly undermine your confidence or focus?

Support Network – Who helps you regain perspective when you feel stuck or overwhelmed?

Commitment to Change – What's one small shift you can make this week to begin restoring your leadership energy?

 **Remember: awareness precedes change.**
You cannot transform what you haven't named.

Worksheet: My Kryptonite to Clarity Plan

Section	Guiding Questions	Your Notes / Actions
1. Kryptonite Identification	What situations or behaviors drain your energy or distract your focus?	
2. Root Cause Analysis	What might be driving these drains (fear, perfectionism, lack of boundaries, unclear goals)?	
3. Antidote Actions	What specific practices or boundaries could counteract each kryptonite source?	
4. Accountability Partner	Who can check in on your progress and encourage consistency?	
5. 28-Day Freedom Plan	Choose one kryptonite area to address over the next 28 days. Write the daily or weekly actions you'll take.	

Quick Checklist

- I have identified at least one personal kryptonite pattern.

- I have written one concrete antidote action I can begin immediately.

- I have shared my goal with an accountability partner or mentor.

- I will revisit this worksheet after 28 days to track progress.

Closing Thought

Every leader has kryptonite. Transformational leadership begins when you decide it will no longer define your limits.

My Kryptonite to Clarity Plan
Chapter Zero - Overcoming the KRYPTONITE Syndrome

Identify Your Kryptonite

What situations, habits, or thoughts consistently drain your leadership energy?

_____

_____

_____

_____

Root Cause Analysis

What might be driving these energy drains (fear, perfectionism, etc.)?

Antidote Actions

What specific practices or boundaries will counter your Kryptonite?

* _____
* _____
* _____

Root Cause Analysis

Who can check in on your progress and encourage consistency?

28-Day Freedom Plan

Choose one kryptonite area to address over the next 28 days. Write the daily or weekly actions you'll take.

1	2	3	4	5	6	7
8	9	10	11	12	13	14
15	16	17	18	19	20	21
22	23	24	25	26	27	28

Quick Checklist

- ◯ I have identified at least one personal kryptonite pattern.
- ◯ I have written one concrete antidote action I can begin immediately.
- ◯ I have shared my goal with an accountability partner or mentor.
- ◯ I will revisit this worksheet after 28 days to track progress.

 **Every leader has kryptonite.**

Transformational leadership begins when you decide it will no longer define your limits.

Understanding Leadership Coaching

Leadership coaching is a transformative process that helps leaders at every level develop self-awareness, clarify goals, and navigate the challenges of leadership. It provides a structured space for reflection, growth, and accountability so that leaders can strengthen both their personal effectiveness and their organizational impact.

For leaders at all stages of responsibility — from team leaders and supervisors to senior executives — coaching offers an opportunity to examine current leadership styles, identify areas for growth, and build strategies that enhance performance. Through one-on-one sessions, leaders are encouraged to reflect on their values, decision-making, and communication patterns. This process deepens self-understanding and allows leaders to recognize how their actions influence teams and organizations.

Leadership coaching is not limited to a single industry or demographic. It is a versatile tool that adapts to the needs of executives, nonprofit leaders, educators, women in leadership, and emerging millennial leaders. While the context may differ, the principles remain consistent: growth requires self-awareness, intentional practice, and a willingness to embrace change.

Ultimately, leadership coaching is about more than professional development — it is about cultivating the mindset and habits that enable leaders to inspire others and foster environments where people thrive.

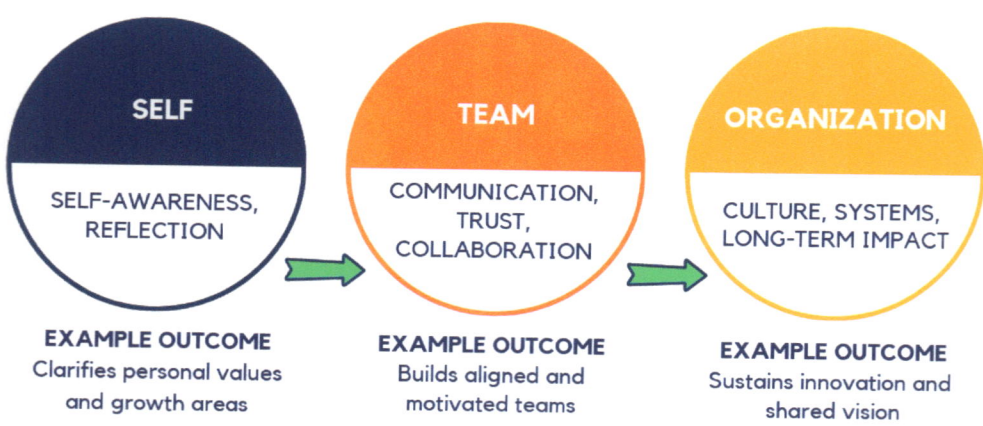

LEADERSHIP COACHING CONTINUUM

Transformational leadership coaching develops the whole leader.

SELF	TEAM	ORGANIZATION
SELF-AWARENESS, REFLECTION	COMMUNICATION, TRUST, COLLABORATION	CULTURE, SYSTEMS, LONG-TERM IMPACT
EXAMPLE OUTCOME Clarifies personal values and growth areas	**EXAMPLE OUTCOME** Builds aligned and motivated teams	**EXAMPLE OUTCOME** Sustains innovation and shared vision

The Importance of Transformational Leadership

In today's complex and rapidly evolving world, the role of a leader extends far beyond managing tasks or meeting short-term goals. Leaders must inspire others, articulate vision, and create cultures where innovation and collaboration can flourish. This is where **transformational leadership** becomes essential.

Transformational leadership is a style that empowers leaders to inspire and influence individuals to reach their full potential. It emphasizes vision, motivation, and creativity, guiding teams to achieve more than they imagined possible. Rather than relying solely on authority, transformational leaders connect with others through authenticity, empathy, and shared purpose.

The benefits extend to both individuals and organizations. For employees, transformational leadership can create a stronger sense of belonging, engagement, and growth. For organizations, it leads to higher levels of innovation, talent retention, and long-term success. In practice, this means not everyone will earn a promotion — but everyone can feel valued, challenged, and integral to the team's mission.

By adopting a transformational approach, leaders create a positive and thriving environment where individuals are motivated to excel. They move beyond simply "getting work done" to fostering cultures of meaning, commitment, and excellence.

Benefits of Transformational Leadership Coaching

Transformational leadership coaching combines the individualized focus of coaching with the broader vision of transformational leadership. Leaders who engage in this type of coaching develop:

- **Self-awareness** — a deeper understanding of strengths, growth areas, and leadership style.

- **Communication and relationship skills** — the ability to listen actively, provide meaningful feedback, and build trust.

- **Strategic thinking** — clarity in decision-making, innovation, and long-range planning.

- **Resilience and adaptability** — tools to remain steady during uncertainty and inspire others to do the same.

Because transformational leadership applies across industries and sectors, this coaching is relevant whether you are guiding a nonprofit team, leading a classroom, managing a corporation, or building an executive career.

Transition to the Fundamentals

While leadership coaching provides a foundation for growth, transformational leadership coaching takes the process further. It equips leaders to not only develop themselves but also to elevate those around them. The next chapter explores the **fundamentals of transformational leadership**, beginning with its definition, the key traits of transformational leaders, and the Four I's that describe how these leaders put their principles into action.

Title: Reframing Leadership at an Urban Public Health Agency

Setting: A city public health department of 600 employees emerging from pandemic response fatigue (2024).

Challenge: Low trust across divisions, rising turnover (18%), and reactive decision-making.

Coaching/Approach: A new deputy commissioner engaged a coach for 6 months, clarified values, crafted a one-paragraph purpose statement, ran 30-day listening tours, and introduced a weekly reflection & planning ritual plus a micro-feedback practice ("one thing to keep/one to improve").

Results: Cross-division project cycle time improved 22%; voluntary turnover dipped to 12%; pulse scores on "I understand our purpose" rose from 48% to 73% within 9 months.

What to Steal: Publish a simple leadership promise + add a visible reflection ritual to reset tone and trust.

COACHING-TO-ACTION CYCLE

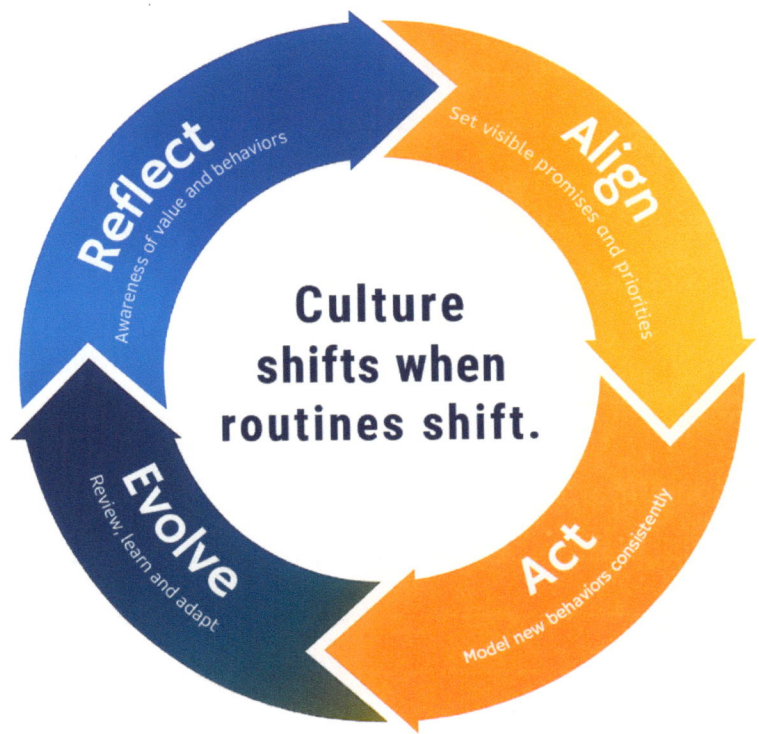

Culture shifts when routines shift.

Reflect — Awareness of value and behaviors

Align — Set visible promises and priorities

Act — Model new behaviors consistently

Evolve — Review, learn and adapt

Conclusion

Transformational leadership begins with self-awareness and intent. Coaching provides the structure for honest reflection, value alignment, and behavior change that others can feel. Leaders who make their promises visible and keep small, steady commitments create the conditions for trust, clarity, and motivation. Culture shifts when routines shift.

Next Steps

- Write a one-paragraph leadership promise that names 3 behaviors you will model.
- Schedule a weekly 45-minute reflection & planning block; protect it like a board meeting.
- Run a 30-day listening tour (15–20 conversations) and publish what you heard + what you'll do.
- Adopt a micro-feedback ritual ("one keep, one improve") with your direct reports.
- Pick 1 trust-building measure (e.g., pulse 'purpose clarity') and track monthly.

Worksheet

Values Clarification
List your top five values. Circle the two you want to amplify at work.

_____

_____

_____

Leadership Promise
Draft your one-paragraph promise. Include 3 observable behaviors.

_____

_____

_____

Stakeholder Map
List 10 key stakeholders (name/role). Note their needs & preferred channel.

_____

_____

_____

90-Day Focus
Name 2 habits to build, 1 habit to stop. Define weekly evidence of progress.

_____

_____

_____

_____

_____

_____

Quick Checklist
☐ I scheduled the key cadences in my calendar.
☐ I identified owners and simple metrics for each action.
☐ I communicated the 'why' and expected outcomes to my team.
☐ I set a 30/60/90 review to assess progress and adjust.

Living on Purpose Prompt: What first step would help you lead yourself more intentionally before leading others?

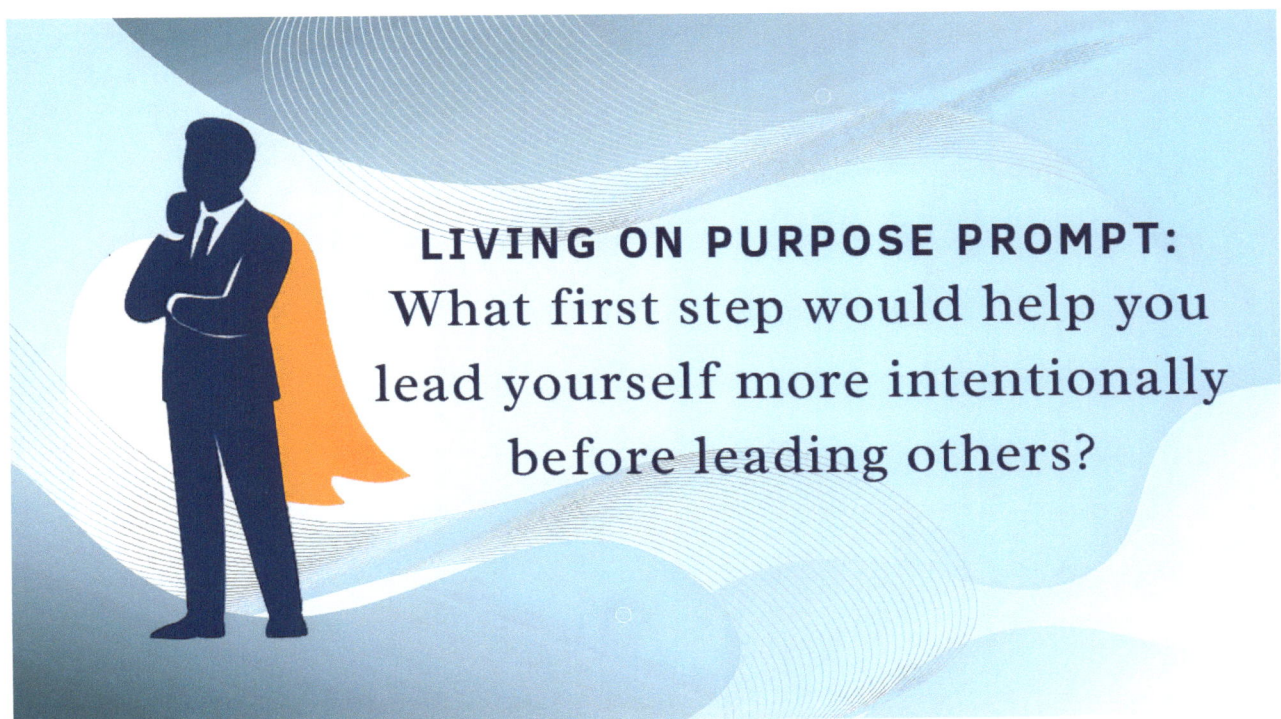

LIVING ON PURPOSE PROMPT: What first step would help you lead yourself more intentionally before leading others?

Chapter 1 Worksheet

Values Clarification

List your top five values. Circle the two you want to amplify at work.

1_____

2_____

3_____

4_____

5_____

Leadership Promise

Draft your one-paragraph promise. Include 3 observable behaviors.

_____

_____

_____

_____

_____

_____

_____

_____

_____

_____

_____

Stakeholder Map

List 10 key stakeholders (name/role). Note their needs & preferred channel.

1. _____
2. _____
3. _____
4. _____
5. _____
6. _____
7. _____
8. _____
9. _____
10. _____

90-Day Focus

Habit to Build

_____

_____

Habit to Build

_____

_____

Month 1—Awareness
Week 4

Month 2—Adjustment
Week 8

Freedom Point
Week 12

Habit to Stop

_____

_____

Quick Checklist

◯	I scheduled the key cadences in my calendar.
◯	I identified owners and simple metrics for each action.
◯	I communicated the 'why' and expected outcomes to my team.
◯	I set a 30/60/90 review to assess progress and adjust.

LIVING ON PURPOSE PROMPT

What first step would help you lead yourself more intentionally before leading others?

Defining Transformational Leadership

In the fast-paced and ever-evolving world of leadership, effectiveness is not measured simply by how well tasks are managed but by how deeply leaders inspire and motivate those around them. Some leaders develop the ability to spark extraordinary results, foster innovation, and strengthen commitment within their organizations. This is the essence of **transformational leadership**.

Transformational leadership goes beyond traditional approaches that focus on oversight and compliance. It emphasizes the personal growth and development of individuals while aligning that growth with the goals of the organization. Transformational leaders cultivate a shared sense of purpose and empower team members to strive for excellence, often surpassing what they thought possible. This approach is not innate; it is learned, practiced, and strengthened over time.

At its core, transformational leadership equips leaders to inspire and influence others toward a collective vision. It requires clarity, communication, and authenticity. By modeling integrity and consistently reinforcing values, transformational leaders help others see themselves as contributors to something greater than their individual roles.

Key Characteristics of Transformational Leaders

Transformational leaders demonstrate qualities that both shape their character and drive their actions. These traits distinguish them from managers who focus only on efficiency or control. They include:

1. **Visionary**: Transformational leaders articulate a compelling vision for the future. They paint a clear picture of success, set ambitious yet achievable goals, and challenge the status quo in pursuit of meaningful progress.

2. **Inspirational**: They inspire confidence in their teams and help people believe in themselves. By leading with authenticity, passion, and integrity, they create environments where enthusiasm and commitment flourish.

3. **Empathetic**: They show genuine concern for their team members, listening actively and supporting both professional and personal growth. Through empathy, they build trust and loyalty that strengthen collaboration.

4. **Development-Oriented**: Transformational leaders are committed to growth. They mentor, coach, and provide feedback, ensuring their team members have opportunities to expand their skills and capabilities.

5. **Change Agents**: They embrace change, encourage innovation, and foster a culture of continuous improvement. They are unafraid to challenge established practices in pursuit of better solutions.

6. **Collaborative**: They value inclusivity and diverse perspectives. By encouraging shared decision-making and collective problem-solving, they create teams that are more engaged and effective.

7. **Resilient**: They remain steady during adversity and model composure for their teams. They view setbacks as opportunities to learn and promote a growth mindset that strengthens long-term success.

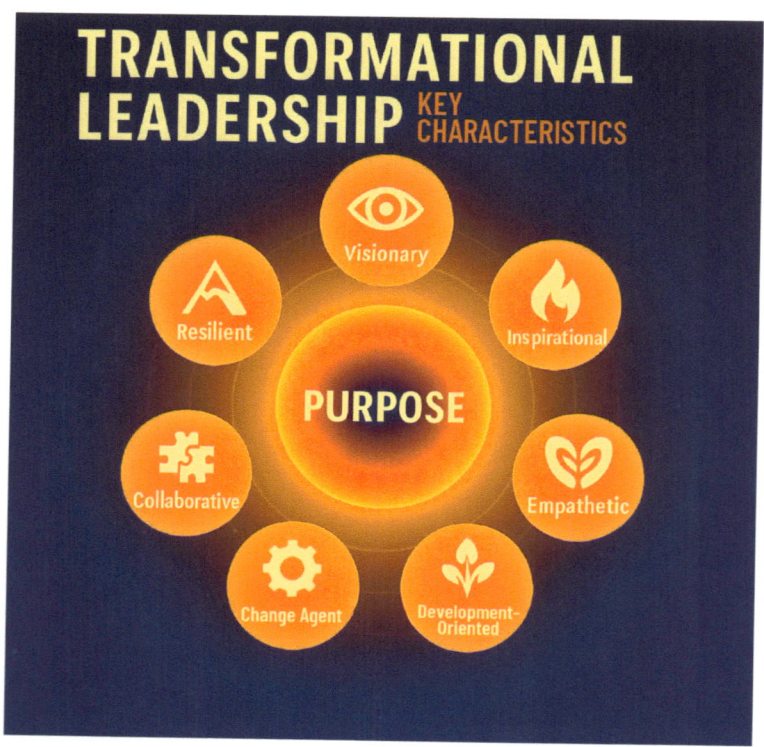

By embodying these characteristics, transformational leaders foster environments where people thrive, innovation takes root, and organizations remain adaptable in changing times.

The Four I's of Transformational Leadership

While traits describe who transformational leaders are, the Four I's describe what they do. These four elements represent the actions that bring transformational leadership to life:

1. **Idealized Influence**: Transformational leaders lead by example. They embody the integrity, honesty, and ethical standards they expect from others. By consistently modeling these values, they earn respect, admiration, and loyalty.

2. **Inspirational Motivation**: They communicate vision with clarity and conviction, inspiring others to embrace shared goals. Their words and actions ignite passion and create a strong sense of purpose across the organization.

3. **Intellectual Stimulation**: They challenge assumptions, encourage creativity, and promote a culture of continuous learning. By asking thought-provoking questions and supporting innovation, they develop critical thinking and adaptability in their teams.

4. **Individualized Consideration**: Transformational leaders recognize the unique strengths and needs of each team member. They provide personalized support, coaching, and opportunities for development, helping individuals grow while contributing meaningfully to the team.

Together, these Four I's translate transformational leadership from concept into practice. They demonstrate how leaders act in ways that inspire trust, empower growth, and deliver lasting impact.

Transition to Leadership Coaching for Executives

Understanding the traits of transformational leaders and the Four I's creates a foundation for applying these principles in real-world leadership. The next chapter explores how transformational leadership coaching helps executives build these qualities and put them into practice at the highest levels of organizational influence.

Modern Case Study

Title: Using the Four I's to Transform a Manufacturing Line

Setting: Mid-market medical device plant (450 staff) with safety incidents and quality escapes (2023–24).

Challenge: "Flavor of the month" initiatives and disengaged operators.

Coaching/Approach: Plant director operationalized the Four I's: daily gemba (Idealized Influence), 2-minute purpose huddles (Inspirational Motivation), 'Fix it in 48' idea sprints (Intellectual Stimulation), and peer coaches for new operators (Individualized Consideration).

Results: Recordable incidents −41%; first-pass yield +5.6 points; 320 frontline ideas implemented in 12 months.

What to Steal: Translate each of the Four I's into a calendar habit with a visible metric.

Conclusion

Traits become culture when they become routines. The Four I's are most powerful as repeatable behaviors—walks, huddles, experiments, and coaching—that compound over time. When people can predict the leader's values in action, they reciprocate with ownership and ideas.

FROM TRAITS TO CULTURE

BEHAVIORS | THE FOUR I's

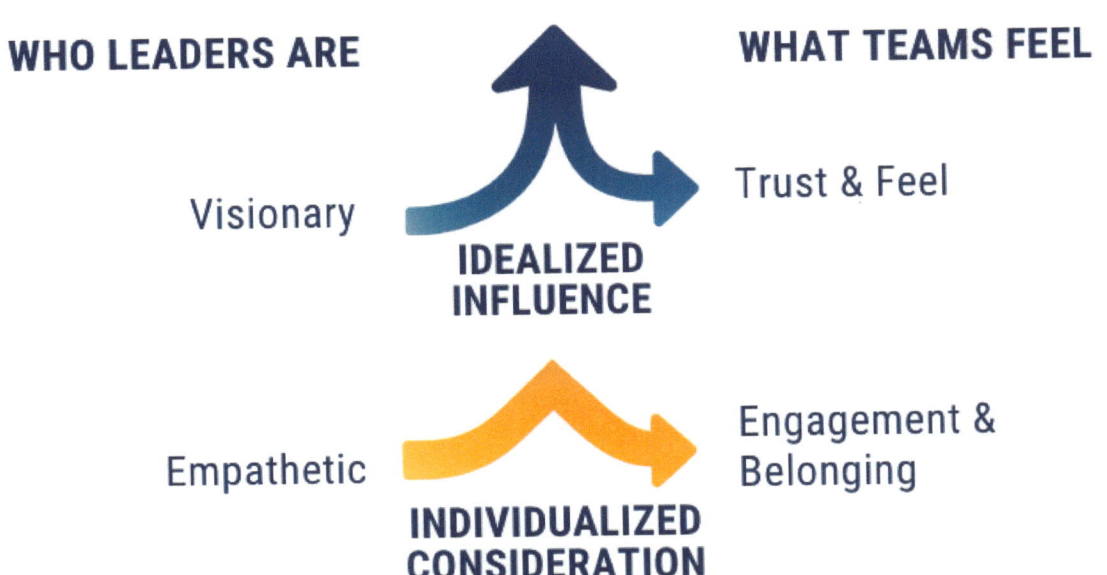

WHO LEADERS ARE

Visionary

IDEALIZED INFLUENCE

Empathetic

INDIVIDUALIZED CONSIDERATION

WHAT TEAMS FEEL

Trust & Feel

Engagement & Belonging

Next Steps

- Map the Four I's to 4 recurring calendar blocks; name the behavior and owner for each.
- Write a 3-sentence vision statement tied to customer or community impact; use in huddles.
- Launch one 30-day idea sprint with a 48-hour decision SLA.
- Assign peer coaches to all new hires for their first 60 days.
- Publish a 'Four I's dashboard' with one behavior metric per I.

Worksheet

The Four I's	Behavior (ritual)	Cadence	Metric / Evidence
Idealized Influence			
Inspirational Motivation			
Intellectual Stimulation			
Individualized Consideration			

Quick Checklist
☐ I scheduled the key cadences in my calendar.
☐ I identified owners and simple metrics for each action.
☐ I communicated the 'why' and expected outcomes to my team.
☐ I set a 30/60/90 review to assess progress and adjust.

Living on Purpose Prompt: Which of your daily leadership habits most reflects your personal purpose — and which one needs realignment?

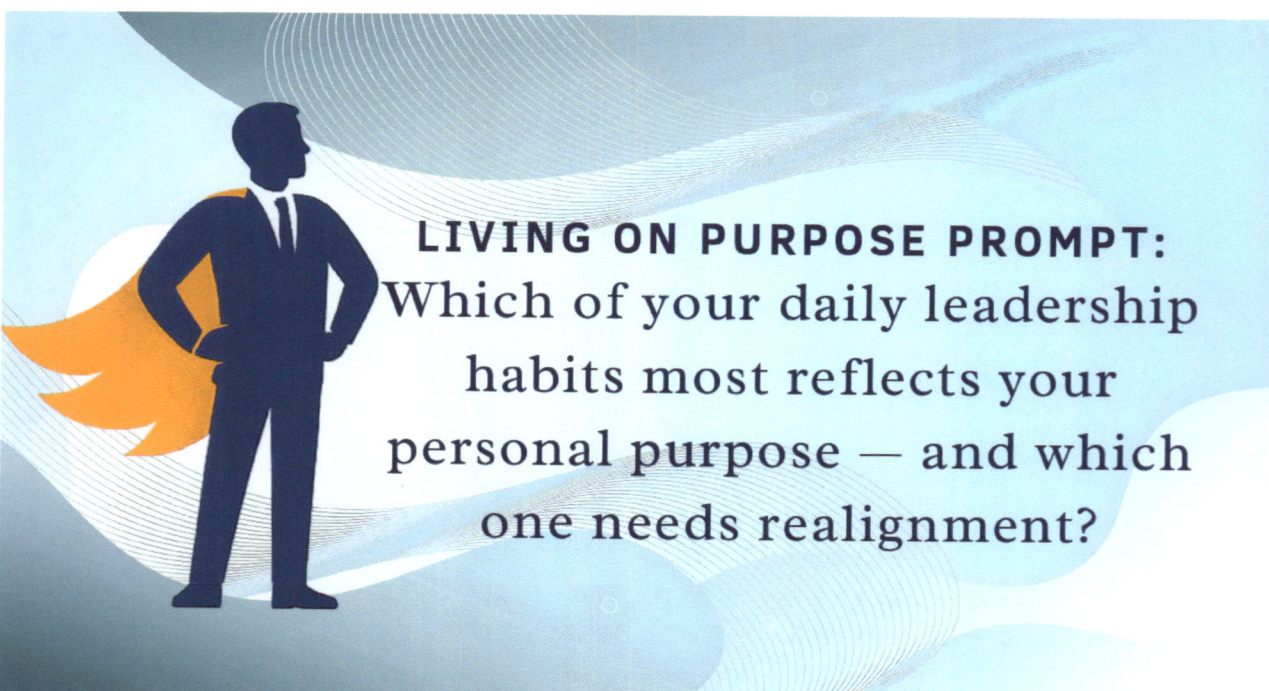

LIVING ON PURPOSE PROMPT: Which of your daily leadership habits most reflects your personal purpose — and which one needs realignment?

Chapter 2 Worksheet

Four I's Dashboard

The Four I's	Behavior (ritual)	Cadence	Metric/Evidence
Inspirational Motivation			
Idealized Influence			
Intellectual Stimulation			
Individualized Consideration			

Quick Checklist

◯	I scheduled the key cadences in my calendar.
◯	I identified owners and simple metrics for each action.
◯	I communicated the 'why' and expected outcomes to my team.
◯	I set a 30/60/90 review to assess progress and adjust.

LIVING ON PURPOSE PROMPT

Which of your daily leadership habits most reflects your personal purpose — and which one needs realignment?

The Role of Executive Leadership Coaching

The path to becoming an exceptional leader is rarely easy. Executives face unique pressures that demand clarity of vision, strong decision-making, and the ability to inspire others while navigating constant change. Executive leadership coaching provides critical support for this journey.

Coaching at this level is a transformative process that enhances skills, strengthens mindset, and builds confidence. It gives leaders a safe and confidential space to reflect on their experiences, confront challenges, and refine their approach. Whether leading a division, an entire organization, or operating in the C-suite, executives benefit from coaching that equips them to make better decisions, inspire trust, and guide their organizations toward sustainable growth.

One of the central roles of executive coaching is to help leaders define and align vision. Through guided reflection and structured dialogue, executives clarify personal values and connect them to organizational purpose. This alignment strengthens authenticity and sharpens strategic focus, creating clarity for both the leader and the teams they guide.

Transformational Coaching Aligns the Inner Work of Leadership with the Outer Impact of Strategy

Assessing and Developing Executive Leadership Skills

Effective leadership begins with self-awareness. By exploring values, motivations, and decision-making styles, leaders gain insight into how their choices affect the organization. This understanding enables them to build on strengths and identify opportunities for growth.

Executive coaching often includes assessments that measure leadership style, personality, or behavioral tendencies. Tools such as 360-degree feedback, personality inventories, and leadership assessments provide valuable data points. These insights form the basis for personalized development plans that target both immediate needs and long-term goals.

Beyond self-assessment, coaching develops essential skills for executive effectiveness:

- **Communication**: honing clarity, listening actively, and delivering feedback that motivates.

- **Strategic Thinking**: analyzing complexity, anticipating challenges, and shaping long-range vision.

- **Decision-Making**: making thoughtful, timely choices even under uncertainty.

- **Emotional Intelligence**: understanding and managing emotions to build trust and strengthen relationships.

These skills are not developed in isolation. They are applied through ongoing coaching conversations, real-time challenges, and reflective practice. This ensures learning translates directly into organizational impact.

EXECUTIVE EFFECTIVENESS FRAMEWORK

**Coaching Strengthens the Core Skills
that Sustain Executive Performance**

Overcoming Challenges in Executive Leadership

Executive leadership brings unique challenges that demand resilience and adaptability. Among the most common are:

- **Leading Diverse Teams**: Executives must foster inclusive environments where different backgrounds and perspectives contribute to innovation. Coaching strengthens skills in cross-cultural communication and inclusive decision-making.

- **Navigating Change**: Market shifts, technological advances, and organizational transitions require leaders to adapt quickly. Coaching provides strategies to reframe change as opportunity and to inspire confidence in times of uncertainty.

- **Balancing Demands**: The weight of responsibility often leads to overextension and burnout. Coaching helps leaders establish boundaries, practice self-care, and model balance for their teams.

- **Addressing Barriers for Women Leaders**: For female executives, gender bias and underrepresentation add another layer of complexity. Coaching equips them with tools for resilience, advocacy, and building supportive networks.

By confronting these challenges with intentional strategies, executives not only strengthen their leadership but also create healthier, more resilient organizations.

Transition to Team Leadership Coaching

Executive coaching builds a foundation of clarity, strategy, and resilience at the highest levels. Yet leadership does not stop at the executive office — it extends to the teams who bring vision to life. The next chapter explores **team leadership coaching**, with a focus on building high-performing teams, fostering collaboration, and inspiring people to achieve shared goals.

Modern Case Study

Title: A New CEO Stabilizes a Fintech Scale-Up

Setting: $120M ARR fintech; founder-CEO steps aside; CFO becomes CEO (2024).

Challenge: Board skepticism, slipping roadmap, and burned-out product teams.

Coaching/Approach: 45-day 360°, decision log for Tier-1 calls, stakeholder map with weekly skip-levels, and calendar rebalanced (40% strategy / 30% people / 20% external / 10% ops).

Results: Roadmap predictability +28%; NPS +12; regrettable attrition −6 points; clean board vote on next round after 9 months.

What to Steal: Visible decision discipline (logs + review dates) builds credibility faster than town halls.

Conclusion

Executive impact hinges on clarity, cadence, and credibility. Coaching helps leaders align time with strategy, make decisions traceable, and strengthen key relationships. When the calendar reflects the vision and decisions are auditable, confidence rises organization-wide.

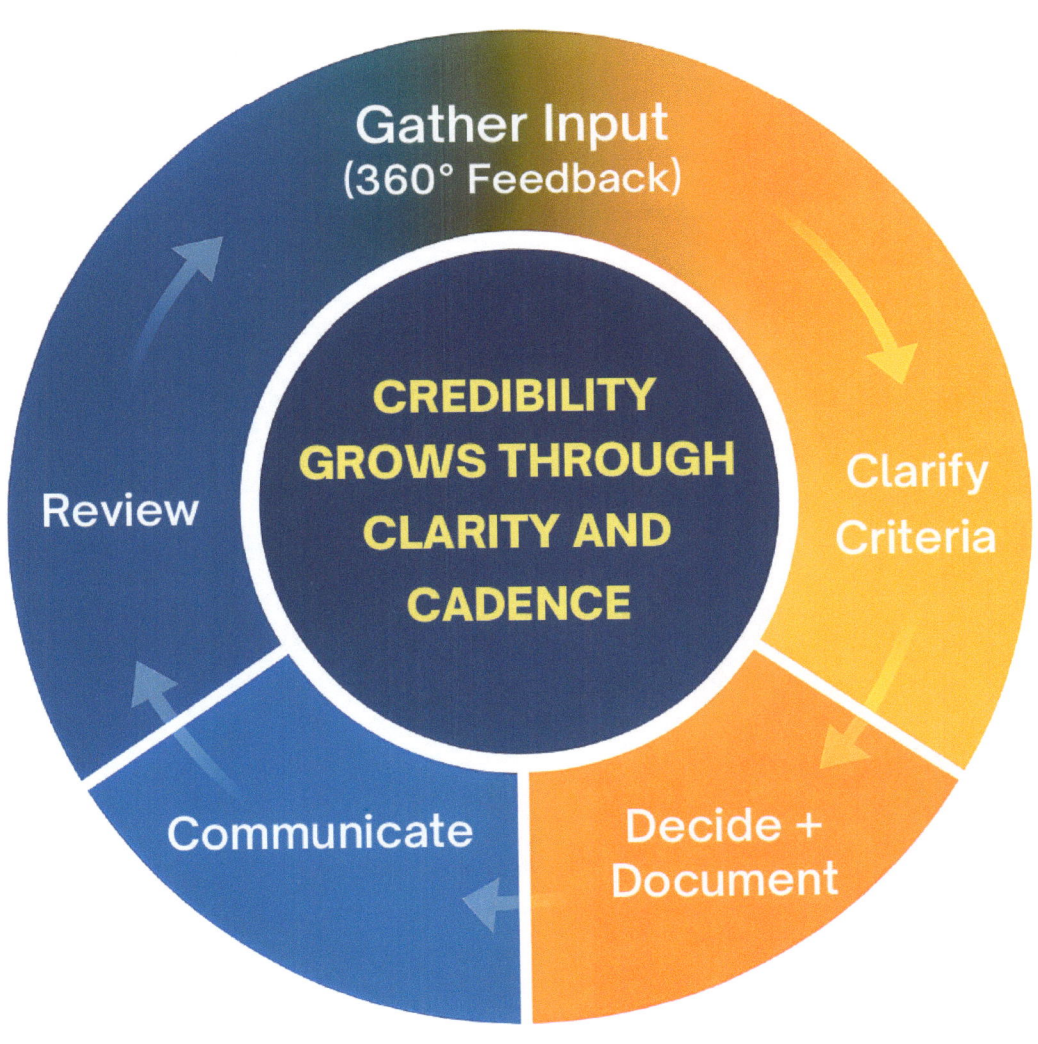

Next Steps

- Run a rapid 360° (interviews + survey) within 45 days; share 3 commitments.
- Create a Tier-1 decision log (owner, options, criteria, decision, review date).
- Audit your calendar; set target allocations for strategy/people/external/ops.
- Map 12 priority stakeholders; schedule quarterly touchpoints now.
- Publish a one-page operating rhythm (meetings, cadences, artifacts).

Worksheet

Stakeholder Priority Map
List top 12 stakeholders; note desired outcomes and cadence.

_____

_____

_____

Decision Log Template
Decision | Context | Options | Criteria | Decision | Review Date | Owner

_____

_____

_____

Calendar Rebalance
Current % vs. Target % for Strategy / People / External / Ops; adjustments.

_____

_____

_____

Quick Checklist

☐ I scheduled the key cadences in my calendar.
☐ I identified owners and simple metrics for each action.
☐ I communicated the 'why' and expected outcomes to my team.
☐ I set a 30/60/90 review to assess progress and adjust.

Living on Purpose Prompt: How does clarifying your personal values strengthen the vision you set for your organization?

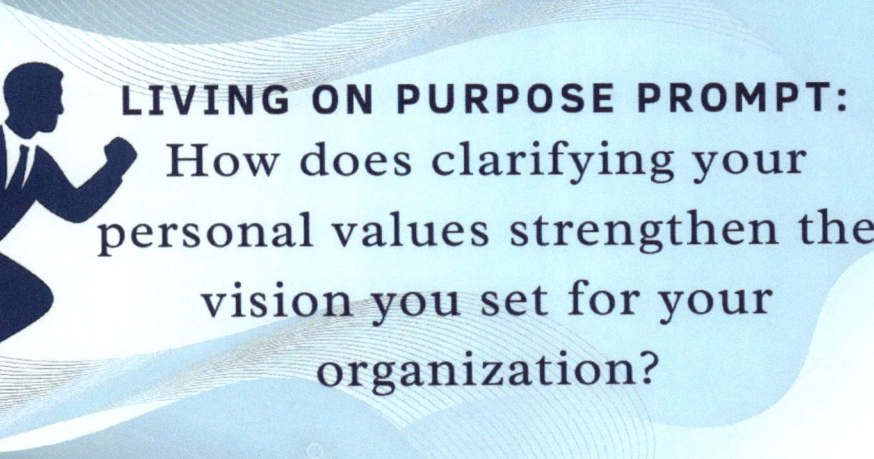

LIVING ON PURPOSE PROMPT:
How does clarifying your personal values strengthen the vision you set for your organization?

Chapter 3 Worksheet

Stakeholder Map

List top 12 stakeholders; note desired outcomes and cadence.

1. _____

_____

2. _____

_____

3. _____

_____

4. _____

_____

5. _____

_____

6. _____

_____

7. _____

_____

8. _____

_____

9. _____

_____

10. _____

_____

11. _____

_____

12. _____

_____

Decision Log

Decision:

Context:

Options:

Criteria:

Final Decision:

Review Date: **Owner:**

Decision:

Context:

Options:

Criteria:

Final Decision:

Review Date: **Owner:**

Decision Log

Decision:

....

....

Context:

....

....

Options:

....

....

Criteria:

....

....

Final Decision:

....

....

Review Date: ....   **Owner:** ....

Calendar Rebalance

CATEGORY	CURRENT %	ADJUSTMENT
STRATEGY		
PEOPLE		
EXTERNAL		
OPERATIONS		

Quick Checklist

○	I scheduled the key cadences in my calendar.
○	I identified owners and simple metrics for each action.
○	I communicated the 'why' and expected outcomes to my team.
○	I set a 30/60/90 review to assess progress and adjust.

LIVING ON PURPOSE PROMPT

How does clarifying your personal values strengthen the vision you set for your organization?

Quick Checklist

◯	I scheduled the key cadences in my calendar.
◯	I identified owners and simple metrics for each action.
◯	I communicated the 'why' and expected outcomes to my team.
◯	I set a 30/60/90 review to assess progress and adjust.

LIVING ON PURPOSE PROMPT

How does clarifying your personal values strengthen the vision you set for your organization?

Chapter 4: Team Leadership Coaching

Building High-Performing Teams

High-performing teams are more than groups of people completing tasks together — they are cohesive units united by purpose, vision, and trust. Leaders who want to develop such teams must be intentional about selection, development, and culture.

Effective team leadership begins with choosing individuals who bring both the skills and the alignment with team values. Yet skill alone is not enough. Leaders must invest in professional development so each team member continues to grow. Transformational coaching supports this by helping leaders identify team strengths, design growth opportunities, and create systems where learning is continuous.

Another essential component is building trust and psychological safety. Teams perform best when members feel safe to share ideas, raise concerns, and take risks without fear of punishment. Leaders foster this by modeling openness, encouraging dialogue, and demonstrating respect for diverse perspectives. When trust is present, collaboration deepens and creativity flourishes.

Finally, effective teams require clarity. Leaders must set shared goals, communicate expectations, and provide the resources needed for success. Progress is sustained through feedback, accountability, and recognition of achievements. Transformational leadership coaching equips leaders with strategies to create this clarity while motivating teams to pursue goals with commitment.

Effective Communication and Collaboration within Teams

Communication is the foundation of collaboration. Leaders must create an environment where every voice can be heard and respected. Active listening demonstrates empathy and validates team contributions. By practicing attentive listening and asking thoughtful questions, leaders signal that input is valued and necessary.

Collaboration goes beyond encouragement; it requires structure. Leaders promote collaboration by creating processes and platforms for brainstorming, problem-solving, and decision-making. Digital tools can support collaboration across distance and time zones, but trust and openness remain the core drivers of effective teamwork.

Clear roles and responsibilities also matter. When individuals understand their contributions in the context of the larger vision, accountability and ownership increase. Regular check-ins and feedback sessions keep goals visible and ensure momentum.

Diversity strengthens collaboration when leaders create inclusive cultures. By valuing differences in background, perspective, and expertise, leaders expand the team's creative potential. Transformational coaching reinforces this by equipping leaders to recognize individual strengths and integrate them into a unified effort.

Motivating and Inspiring Team Members

Motivation drives performance, but inspiration sustains it. Transformational leaders do more than set targets — they help team members find meaning in their work. This involves understanding individual aspirations, connecting tasks to broader goals, and showing team members how their contributions matter.

Practical motivational strategies include recognizing achievements, offering constructive feedback, and providing growth opportunities. Yet true inspiration taps into emotion and purpose. Leaders who share stories, model passion, and connect vision to daily work ignite energy that goes beyond compliance.

Creating a motivating environment also means fostering inclusion and belonging. When team members feel respected and supported, they are more likely to commit fully and take ownership of outcomes. Transformational coaching helps leaders build these environments by teaching them to combine empathy, vision, and accountability in ways that resonate with their teams.

	MOTIVATION	INSPIRATION
	Task-Focused	Purpose-Focused
External Drivers	Rewards / Recognition 🏅	Shared Vision ⭐
Internal Drivers	Growth Opportunities 📈	Meaning & Belonging 💛
	Motivation sparks effort.	Inspiration sustains excellence.

Transition to Women in Leadership Coaching

Team leadership coaching equips leaders with skills to build trust, foster collaboration, and inspire performance across diverse groups. The next chapter turns to a more focused challenge — supporting women in leadership. Chapter 5 explores how coaching can address bias, empower women, and create pathways for advancement in leadership roles.

Modern Case Study

Title: Making a Hybrid Product Team High-Performing

Setting: Global SaaS team across 5 time zones (2025).

Challenge: Meetings overloaded with status, unclear ownership, and missed hand-offs.

Coaching/Approach: Co-created a one-page team charter, replaced status meetings with a live dashboard, added monthly retros, and implemented a RACI for releases.

Results: Lead time −23%; sprint predictability +19%; team safety score rose from 6.4 to 8.1/10 in 6 months.

What to Steal: Charter + dashboard + retro = the modern operating system for distributed teams.

Conclusion

High-performing teams don't happen by accident—they are designed. Clear purpose, decision rights, transparent work, and regular learning loops convert energy into outcomes. The leader's role is to set the system, not to sit in every meeting.

Next Steps

- Draft a one-page charter (purpose, outcomes, norms, decision rights).
- Replace weekly status with a living dashboard; keep meetings for decisions.
- Run monthly retros with 2 actions max; track completion.
- Create a RACI for your critical workflow; publish it in your tool of record.
- Institutionalize onboarding: assign a buddy + 30/60/90 plan.

Worksheet

Team Charter
Purpose | Top 3 outcomes | Working norms | Decision rights | Tools

_____

_____

_____

_____

_____

RACI Sketch
List 5 key steps; mark R/A/C/I per role.

_____

_____

_____

Retro Kit
What to start/stop/continue; 2 action items; owners & due dates.

_____

_____

_____

Quick Checklist
☐ I scheduled the key cadences in my calendar.
☐ I identified owners and simple metrics for each action.
☐ I communicated the 'why' and expected outcomes to my team.
☐ I set a 30/60/90 review to assess progress and adjust.

Living on Purpose Prompt: How can leading on purpose help you build a team culture grounded in trust and shared accountability?

LIVING ON PURPOSE PROMPT:
How can leading on purpose help you build a team culture grounded in trust and shared accountability?

Chapter 4 Worksheet

TEAM CHARTER

PURPOSE

TOP 3 OUTCOMES

1 ....

2 ....

3 ....

WORKING NORMS

DECISION RIGHTS

TOOLS

RACI SKETCH

Mark responsibility per role; clarity builds accountability.

STEP	R	A	C	I

RETRO KIT

Small adjustments compound into team transformation.

START	STOP	CONTINUE

ACTION ITEM	OWNER/DUE DATE

Quick Checklist

◯	I scheduled the key cadences in my calendar.
◯	I identified owners and simple metrics for each action.
◯	I communicated the 'why' and expected outcomes to my team.
◯	I set a 30/60/90 review to assess progress and adjust.

LIVING ON PURPOSE PROMPT

How can leading on purpose help you build a team culture grounded in trust and shared accountability?

Chapter 5: Women in Leadership Coaching

Addressing Gender Bias in Leadership

Gender bias — whether conscious or unconscious — continues to shape decision-making, opportunities, and culture in organizations. These biases limit access to advancement, narrow perspectives, and undermine organizational effectiveness. Leaders who wish to create truly inclusive environments must recognize bias, understand how it manifests, and take intentional steps to address it.

Transformational leadership coaching provides tools for building this awareness. Through reflection and feedback, leaders uncover blind spots, examine assumptions, and strengthen their ability to make equitable decisions. Coaching also equips leaders with strategies to interrupt bias in hiring, performance evaluation, and promotion processes. By developing these skills, leaders become advocates for fairness while modeling inclusion for their teams.

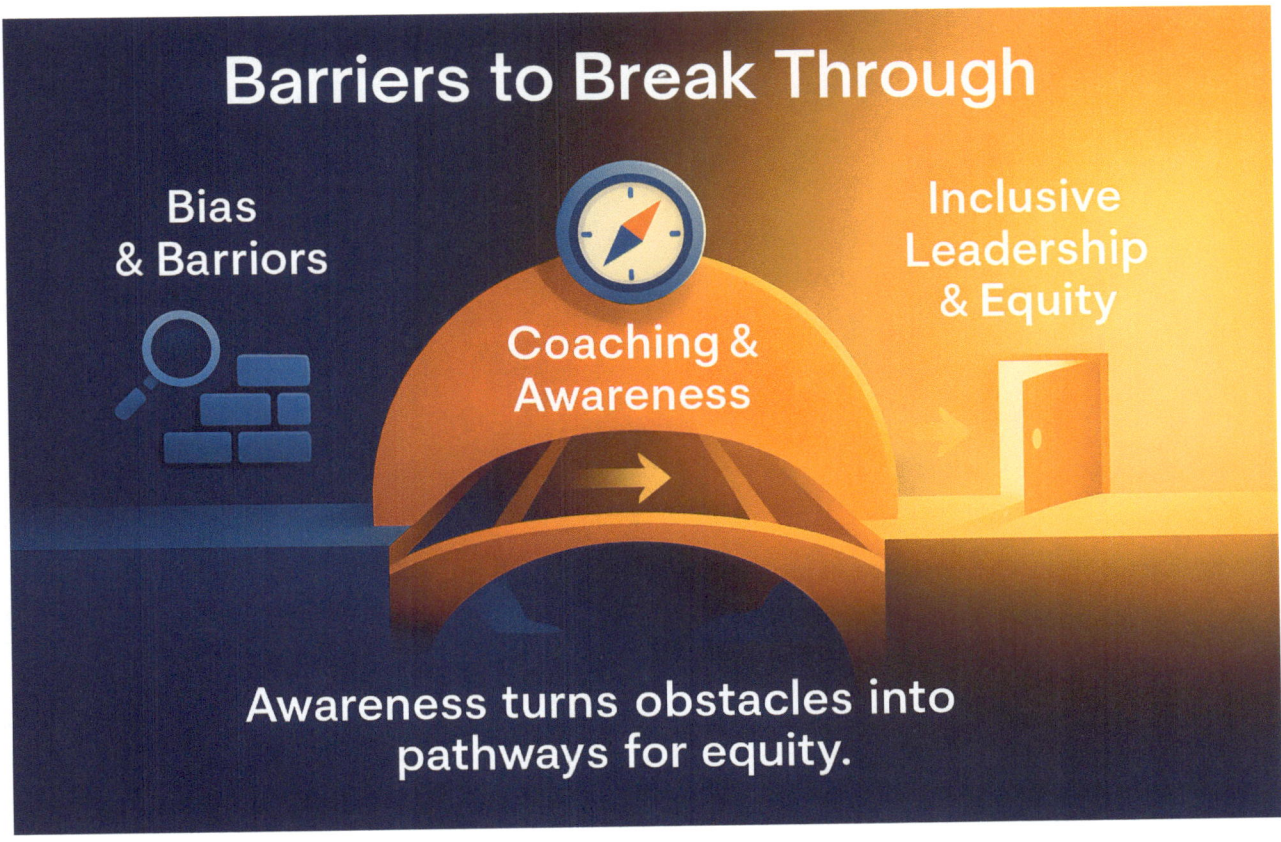

Empowering Women Leaders

Organizations increasingly recognize the value women bring to leadership roles. Women contribute diverse perspectives, relational insight, and collaborative approaches that drive innovation and resilience. Yet barriers remain, including underrepresentation in senior roles, limited access to networks, and cultural expectations around work-life balance.

Transformational coaching empowers women to overcome these barriers by building confidence, clarifying purpose, and strengthening advocacy skills. Coaches support women in developing strategies for negotiation, visibility, and influence. They also help leaders navigate bias with resilience, ensuring that challenges become opportunities for growth rather than roadblocks.

Equally important, coaching reinforces the power of networks and mentorship. By connecting women to mentors and sponsors, leaders expand their access to guidance and advocacy. Sponsorship, in particular, ensures that women are not only supported but also championed for advancement opportunities.

Strategies for Advancing Women in Leadership Roles

Progress requires more than individual effort — it depends on organizational commitment to equity. Transformational leaders can drive this progress through specific strategies:

1. **Create Inclusive Cultures**: Foster environments where women's voices are heard and valued. Implement policies that support work-life balance, flexible scheduling, and equal pay. Build systems that reward inclusive behavior, not just individual achievement.

2. **Mentorship and Sponsorship**: Establish structured programs that connect women to mentors for guidance and sponsors for advocacy. Sponsors play a crucial role in opening doors to leadership opportunities.

3. **Targeted Development**: Offer leadership development programs that prepare women for advancement, with training in strategic thinking, communication, and negotiation, as well as opportunities to expand networks.

4. **Accountability**: Track representation, advancement rates, and pay equity. Hold leaders accountable for progress, just as they are accountable for financial or operational results.

By implementing these practices, organizations unlock the full potential of women leaders and strengthen overall performance.

STRATEGIES TO ADVANCE WOMEN IN LEADERSHIP

Inclusive Cultures

Policies that support balance

Mentorship & Sponsorship

Programs that connect advocates

Targeted Development

Training that expands opportunities

Accountability

Metrics that ensures progress

Equity grows when culture, connection, development, and accountability align.

Transition to Nonprofit Leadership Coaching

Coaching that empowers women highlights how transformational leadership adapts to specific challenges and contexts. The next chapter examines another unique leadership environment — the nonprofit sector — where resource constraints, complex stakeholder relationships, and mission-driven goals demand a distinct application of transformational leadership coaching.

Modern Case Study

Title: From Senior Director to VP—With Sponsorship and System Change

Setting: National healthcare nonprofit (2024).

Challenge: High-performing woman stalled at VP threshold; pay inequities in banding.

Coaching/Approach: Built a personal board (mentor/sponsor/peer coach), crafted a negotiation brief, and piloted structured interviews + transparent salary bands in her division.

Results: Promotion to VP; 11% pay equity correction; time-to-fill −20% with diverse slates maintained.

What to Steal: Pair individual agency with one systemic fix you control.

Conclusion

Equity advances when individuals are equipped and systems evolve. Coaching builds confidence, strategy, and voice—while leaders also adjust processes that create fairer outcomes. Sponsorship turns potential into opportunity.

Next Steps

- Assemble a 'personal board' (mentor, sponsor, peer coach) with explicit asks.
- Draft a negotiation brief (market data, impact, options, walk-away).
- Pilot bias interrupters in one process (hiring, promotion, calibration).
- Create a visibility plan (panels, projects, publications) for 90 days.
- Track 3 equity metrics (representation, promotion rate, pay bands).

Worksheet

Personal Board Canvas
Name | Role | What I need | Next touchpoint

_____

_____

_____

_____

_____

Negotiation Brief
My ask | Evidence | Alternatives | Concessions | Walk-away

_____

_____

_____

_____

Bias Interrupters Checklist
Structured interview? Diverse slate? Criteria defined pre-screen? Salary bands posted?

_____

_____

_____

_____

_____

_____

Quick Checklist
☐ I scheduled the key cadences in my calendar.
☐ I identified owners and simple metrics for each action.
☐ I communicated the 'why' and expected outcomes to my team.
☐ I set a 30/60/90 review to assess progress and adjust.

Living on Purpose Prompt: How does living on purpose empower you — and those you mentor — to lead with confidence and equity?

LIVING ON PURPOSE PROMPT: How does living on purpose empower you — and those you mentor — to lead with confidence and equity?

Chapter 5 Worksheet

PERSONAL BOARD CANVAS

NAME

ROLE

WHAT I NEED

NEXT TOUCHPOINT

NAME

ROLE

WHAT I NEED

NEXT TOUCHPOINT

NAME

ROLE

WHAT I NEED

NEXT TOUCHPOINT

NEGOTIATION BRIEF

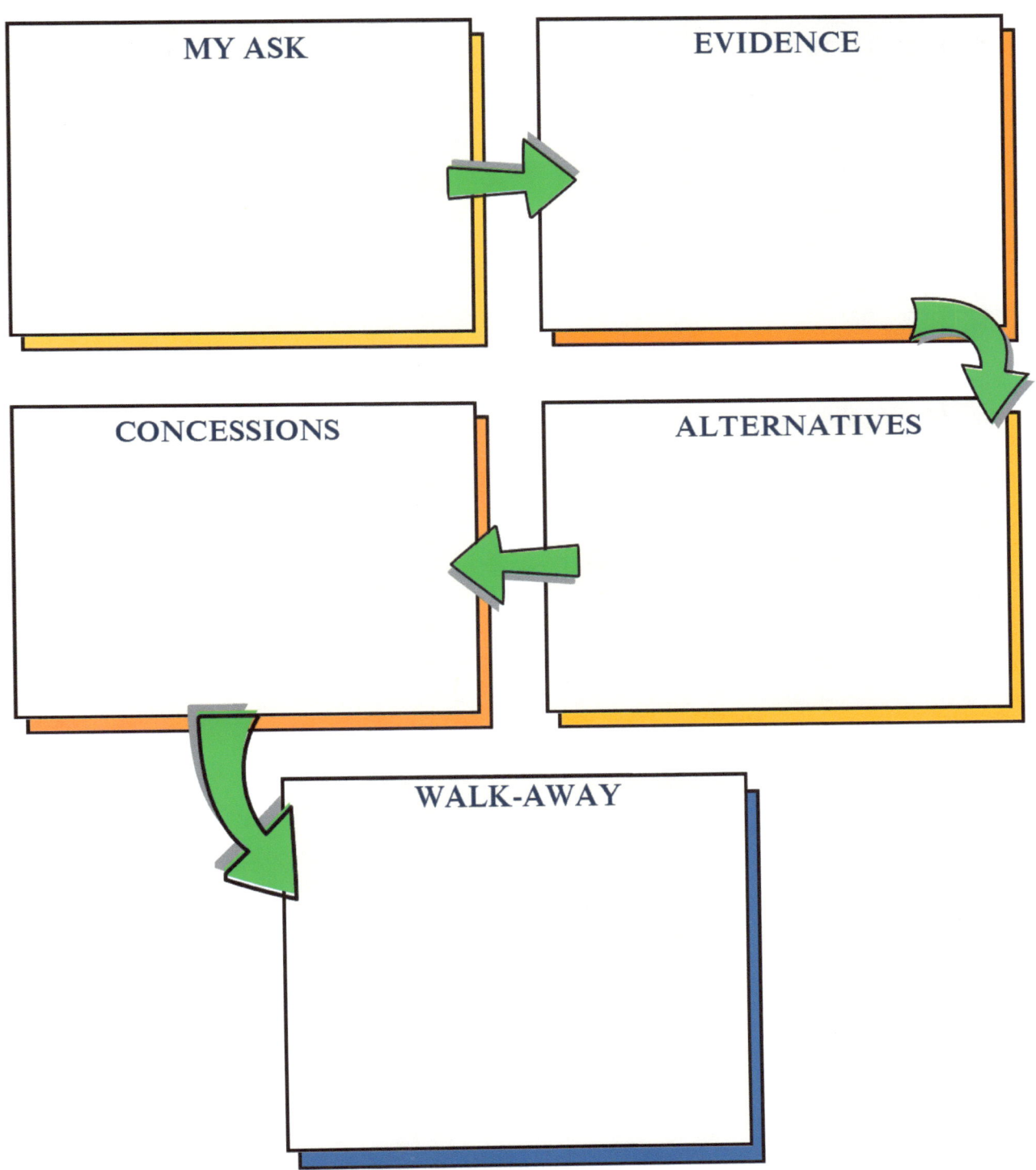

MY ASK

EVIDENCE

CONCESSIONS

ALTERNATIVES

WALK-AWAY

BIAS INTERRUPTERS CHECKLIST

✓	QUESTIONS/PRACTICE	NOTES/FOLLOW-UP ACTION
◯	Are interviews structured with consistent questions?	
◯	Was a diverse candidate slate considered?	
◯	Were selection criteria defined before screening?	
◯	Are salary bands transparent and posted?	
◯	Was feedback reviewed for language bias (e.g., "aggressive," "emotional")?	
◯	Were multiple reviewers involved to reduce confirmation bias?	
◯	Are development opportunities equitably distributed?	

Quick Checklist

○	I scheduled the key cadences in my calendar.
○	I identified owners and simple metrics for each action.
○	I communicated the 'why' and expected outcomes to my team.
○	I set a 30/60/90 review to assess progress and adjust.

LIVING ON PURPOSE PROMPT

How does living on purpose empower you — and those you mentor — to lead with confidence and equity?

Understanding the Unique Challenges of Nonprofit Leadership

Nonprofit leaders carry responsibilities that extend beyond financial results. They must balance limited resources, meet the expectations of diverse stakeholders, and remain faithful to mission-driven goals. These challenges often require navigating competing priorities, such as ensuring financial sustainability while delivering community impact.

Transformational leadership coaching equips nonprofit leaders to thrive within this complexity. It provides tools for clarifying vision, aligning staff and volunteers around mission, and communicating effectively with funders, boards, and community partners. By strengthening skills in adaptability, resourcefulness, and collaboration, coaching enables nonprofit leaders to maximize impact even when resources are constrained.

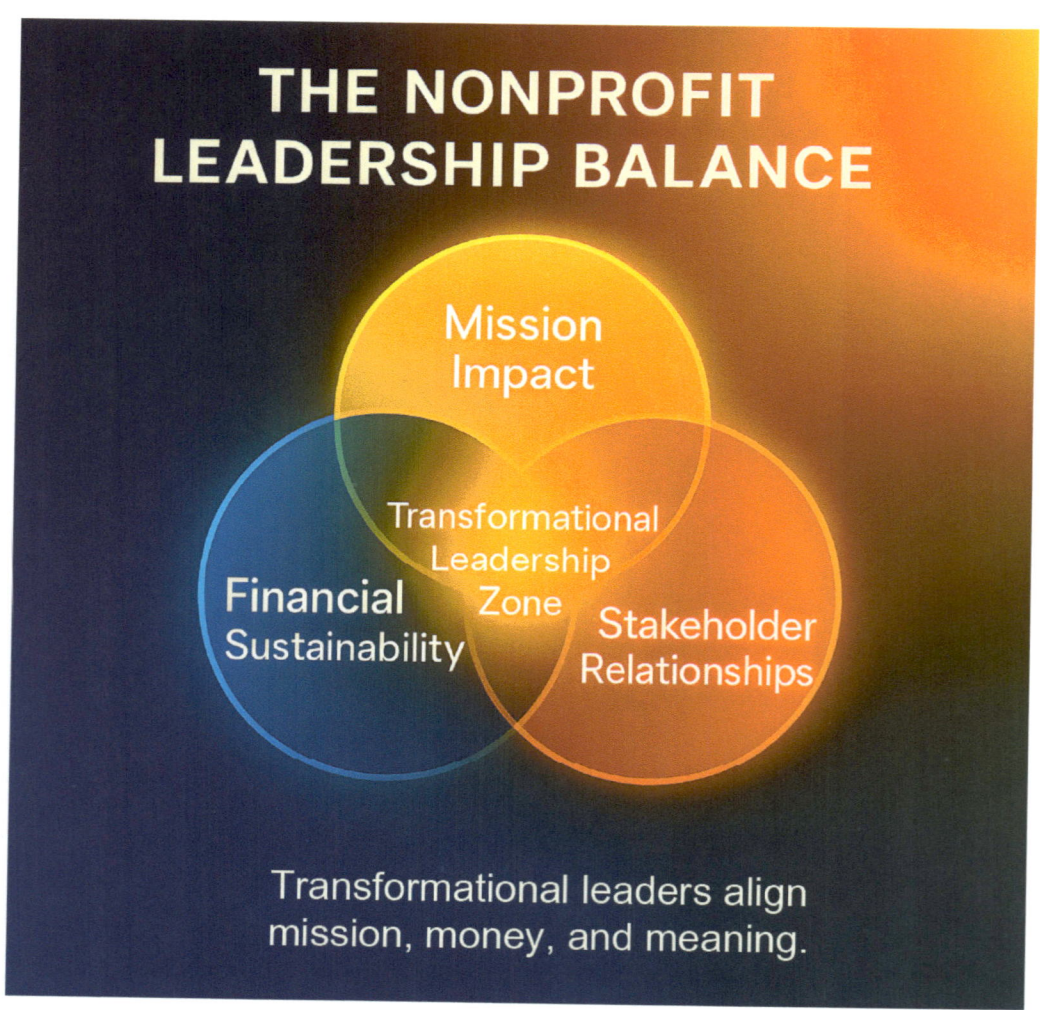

THE NONPROFIT LEADERSHIP BALANCE

Mission Impact

Transformational Leadership Zone

Financial Sustainability

Stakeholder Relationships

Transformational leaders align mission, money, and meaning.

Applying Transformational Leadership Principles in Nonprofit Settings

Transformational leadership principles are especially powerful in nonprofits, where the ability to inspire others often compensates for limited material resources. Nonprofit leaders who embrace transformational coaching practices:

- **Communicate Vision**: They consistently connect daily work to the broader mission, helping staff and volunteers see meaning in their contributions.

- **Foster Innovation**: They encourage creative solutions for persistent challenges, such as funding gaps or service expansion, and celebrate experimentation as a path to growth.

- **Empower Teams**: They invest in developing both staff and volunteers, providing mentorship and recognition that cultivate loyalty and energy.

- **Build Trust**: They strengthen credibility with boards, funders, and communities by modeling transparency, accountability, and integrity.

Coaching helps leaders translate these principles into daily practice. Through guided reflection and accountability, nonprofit leaders learn to balance strategic planning with empathy, ensuring decisions reflect both organizational needs and community values.

Creating a Culture of Impact and Engagement

Sustaining nonprofit work requires more than vision — it requires cultures where people feel inspired to contribute their time, resources, and expertise. Transformational coaching helps leaders design such cultures by teaching them to recognize contributions, celebrate progress, and cultivate belonging.

When staff and volunteers feel connected to mission and valued as individuals, their commitment deepens. This engagement drives stronger program outcomes, higher donor trust, and long-term sustainability. By embedding transformational leadership practices into their organizations, nonprofit leaders create environments where passion for the mission translates into tangible results.

CULTURE OF IMPACT DASHBOARD

Program Reach · Client Satisfaction · Funding Stability · Volunteer Retention

Shared metrics transform passion into measurable progress.

Transition to Leadership Coaching for Millennials

The nonprofit context demonstrates how transformational leadership adapts to different environments. Another critical context is generational leadership, particularly for millennials, who now make up a significant portion of the workforce. Chapter 7 explores how transformational leadership coaching can address the unique expectations and strengths of millennial leaders, while offering principles relevant to all generations.

Modern Case Study

Title: From Programs to Impact at a Food Justice Nonprofit

Setting: $6M community nonprofit expanding into two neighborhoods (2023–24).

Challenge: Funder fatigue; impact stories without common metrics.

Coaching/Approach: Rebuilt logic model, launched a 5-metric impact dashboard, and ran a 90-day innovation sprint on mobile pantry scheduling.

Results: On-time pantry visits +31%; client return rate +18%; two multi-year grants ($1.2M) citing clear outcomes.

What to Steal: A simple, shared dashboard aligns staff pride with funder confidence.

Conclusion

Mission becomes momentum when impact is measurable. Coaching helps leaders translate passion into shared definitions of success, continuous improvement, and compelling narratives for staff, boards, and funders.

Next Steps

- Draft a one-page logic model (inputs → activities → outputs → outcomes).
- Select 5 organization-level metrics; set definitions and owners.
- Publish a monthly impact dashboard to staff and board.
- Run one 90-day innovation sprint on a service bottleneck.
- Create a donor 'impact story' template with before/after evidence.

Worksheet

Logic Model Element	Your Notes
Inputs (resources)	
Activities (what you do)	
Outputs (volume)	
Short-term outcomes (3–12 mo)	
Long-term outcomes (12–36 mo)	

Quick Checklist
☐ I scheduled the key cadences in my calendar.
☐ I identified owners and simple metrics for each action.
☐ I communicated the 'why' and expected outcomes to my team.
☐ I set a 30/60/90 review to assess progress and adjust.

Living on Purpose Prompt: In what ways can purposeful leadership help your team stay aligned with mission when resources are limited?

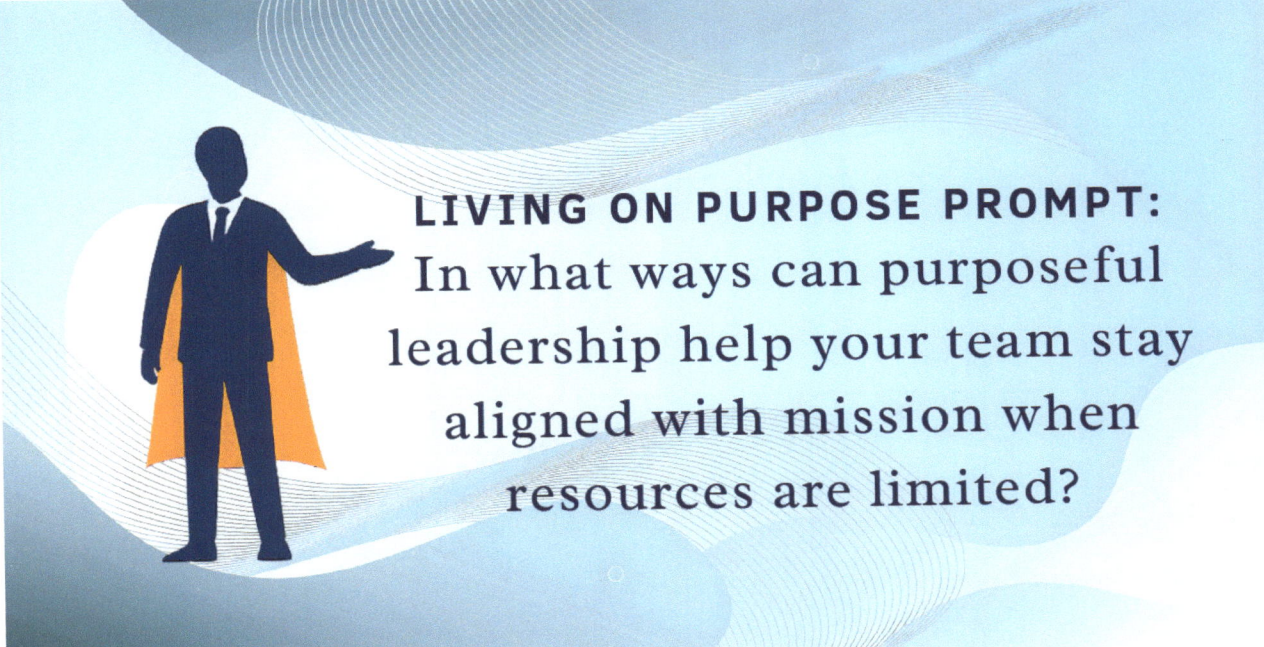

LIVING ON PURPOSE PROMPT: In what ways can purposeful leadership help your team stay aligned with mission when resources are limited?

Chapter 6 Worksheet

Logic Model Element	Your Notes
Inputs (resources)	
Activities (what you do)	
Outputs (volume)	
Short-term outcomes (3–12 mo)	
Long-term outcomes (12–36 mo)	

Impact Planning Toolkit

INPUTS	ACTIVITIES	OUTPUTS	OUTCOMES	IMPACT

Impact Story Template

BEFORE	CHALLENGE	INTERVENTION	RESULT

Quick Checklist

◯	I scheduled the key cadences in my calendar.
◯	I identified owners and simple metrics for each action.
◯	I communicated the 'why' and expected outcomes to my team.
◯	I set a 30/60/90 review to assess progress and adjust.

LIVING ON PURPOSE PROMPT

In what ways can purposeful leadership help your team stay aligned with mission when resources are limited?

Chapter 7: Leadership Coaching for Millennials

Understanding Millennial Leadership Styles

Millennials now represent a large share of the global workforce, and many are stepping into leadership roles. They bring unique perspectives shaped by digital fluency, collaboration, and a strong desire for purpose-driven work. While these traits are often associated with millennials, the underlying themes—flexibility, inclusivity, and meaning—resonate across generations.

Transformational leadership coaching provides a framework for engaging these values productively. Rather than labeling leadership by generation, coaching emphasizes principles that meet people where they are, encouraging adaptability, emotional intelligence, and authenticity. For millennial leaders, this often means leveraging collaboration, openness, and innovation while learning to balance those qualities with accountability and long-term vision.

Developing Millennial Leaders

Coaching supports millennial leaders in translating potential into impact. Key areas of focus include:

- **Clarifying Purpose**: Many millennials seek meaning in their work. Coaching helps them define personal values and align those values with organizational mission.

- **Strengthening Communication**: Coaching develops the ability to communicate across generations and styles, ensuring messages resonate with diverse teams.

- **Building Resilience**: Millennials entering leadership often face skepticism or bias. Coaching equips them with confidence, perseverance, and strategies to overcome obstacles.

- **Expanding Strategic Thinking**: Coaching challenges millennial leaders to move beyond immediate tasks and consider long-term impact, risk, and organizational strategy.

By emphasizing both strengths and growth areas, transformational coaching creates pathways for millennial leaders to inspire trust and earn credibility.

Nurturing a Multigenerational Work Environment

The modern workplace is not only millennial; it is multigenerational. Baby Boomers, Gen X, Millennials, and Gen Z often work side by side, each bringing different strengths and expectations. Effective leadership requires creating environments where these differences become assets rather than sources of conflict.

Transformational coaching helps leaders—millennials and others—build cultures of respect, collaboration, and inclusion. Leaders learn to value diverse perspectives, bridge communication gaps, and foster shared purpose across age groups. This approach ensures that generational differences strengthen organizations instead of dividing them.

Transition to Educational Leadership Coaching

Millennial leadership demonstrates how coaching adapts to generational strengths and challenges, while offering lessons for all leaders in fostering adaptability and inclusion. The next chapter examines transformational leadership coaching in education—where vision, emotional intelligence, and inclusivity shape how schools and institutions prepare the next generation of leaders.

Modern Case Study

Title: Purpose-Led Ops in a Multigenerational Hospital Unit

Setting: Millennial director leading 120-person hospital support unit (2025).

Challenge: Cross-gen friction; high churn among early-career staff.

Coaching/Approach: Co-created a purpose statement, instituted micro-feedback, formed cross-gen advisory circles, and ran quarterly 'experiments with a metric.'

Results: Early-career retention +14 points; patient satisfaction +9%; 'I feel heard' +21 points.

What to Steal: Purpose + feedback rituals + small experiments = performance.

Conclusion

Generational diversity is an advantage when purpose is shared and voices are heard. Coaching equips leaders to turn values into practices that bridge styles, reduce friction, and accelerate learning.

Next Steps

- Write and test a one-sentence team purpose; post it where work happens.
- Start a fortnightly micro-feedback loop (ask/offer/commit).
- Launch a cross-gen advisory circle (6–8 staff) with rotating facilitation.
- Create a quarterly experiment backlog with one metric per test.
- Celebrate learning, not just wins; debrief 'what we tried/what we learned.'

Worksheet

Purpose Canvas
Draft, test with team, refine to one sentence.

_____

_____

_____

Communication Styles Map
List preferences across 4–5 team members; note bridges/risks.

_____

_____

_____

Experiment Backlog
Idea | Hypothesis | Metric | Owner | Sprint window

_____

_____

_____

Quick Checklist
☐ I scheduled the key cadences in my calendar.
☐ I identified owners and simple metrics for each action.
☐ I communicated the 'why' and expected outcomes to my team.
☐ I set a 30/60/90 review to assess progress and adjust.

Living on Purpose Prompt: How does aligning purpose with performance help you inspire others across generations?

Chapter 7 Worksheet

PURPOSE + FEEDBACK LOOP

STEP	ACTION	NOTES
DEFINE	Write a one-sentence team purpose.	
ASK	What's one thing that helped you succeed this week?	
OFFER	What's one way I can support you better?	
COMMIT	Note one change to test in the next two weeks.	

COMMUNICATIONS STYLES MAP

TEAM MEMBER	PREFERRED STYLE	STRENGTHS	BRIDGES/ RISKS
John W.	Direct / Analytical	Clear, efficient	May seem abrupt

EXPERIMENT BACKLOG

IDEA

HYPOTHESIS

METRIC

OWNER

SPRINT WINDOW

IDEA

HYPOTHESIS

METRIC

OWNER

SPRINT WINDOW

EXPERIMENT BACKLOG

IDEA

HYPOTHESIS

METRIC

OWNER

SPRINT WINDOW

IDEA

HYPOTHESIS

METRIC

OWNER

SPRINT WINDOW

Quick Checklist

◯	I scheduled the key cadences in my calendar.
◯	I identified owners and simple metrics for each action.
◯	I communicated the 'why' and expected outcomes to my team.
◯	I set a 30/60/90 review to assess progress and adjust.

LIVING ON PURPOSE PROMPT

How does aligning purpose with performance help you inspire others across generations?

The Role of Leadership in Education

Educational institutions shape the next generation of citizens and leaders. The quality of leadership in schools, colleges, and universities directly influences not only academic outcomes but also the culture of learning and growth within communities. Unlike corporate leadership, where profit and performance often dominate, educational leadership is rooted in vision, inclusivity, and long-term development.

Transformational leadership coaching supports educational leaders—principals, department chairs, administrators, and teacher-leaders—in balancing these responsibilities. Coaching helps them articulate vision, build strong school cultures, and inspire staff and students to achieve their best. By focusing on both personal growth and systemic impact, coaching equips leaders to guide institutions through the challenges of modern education.

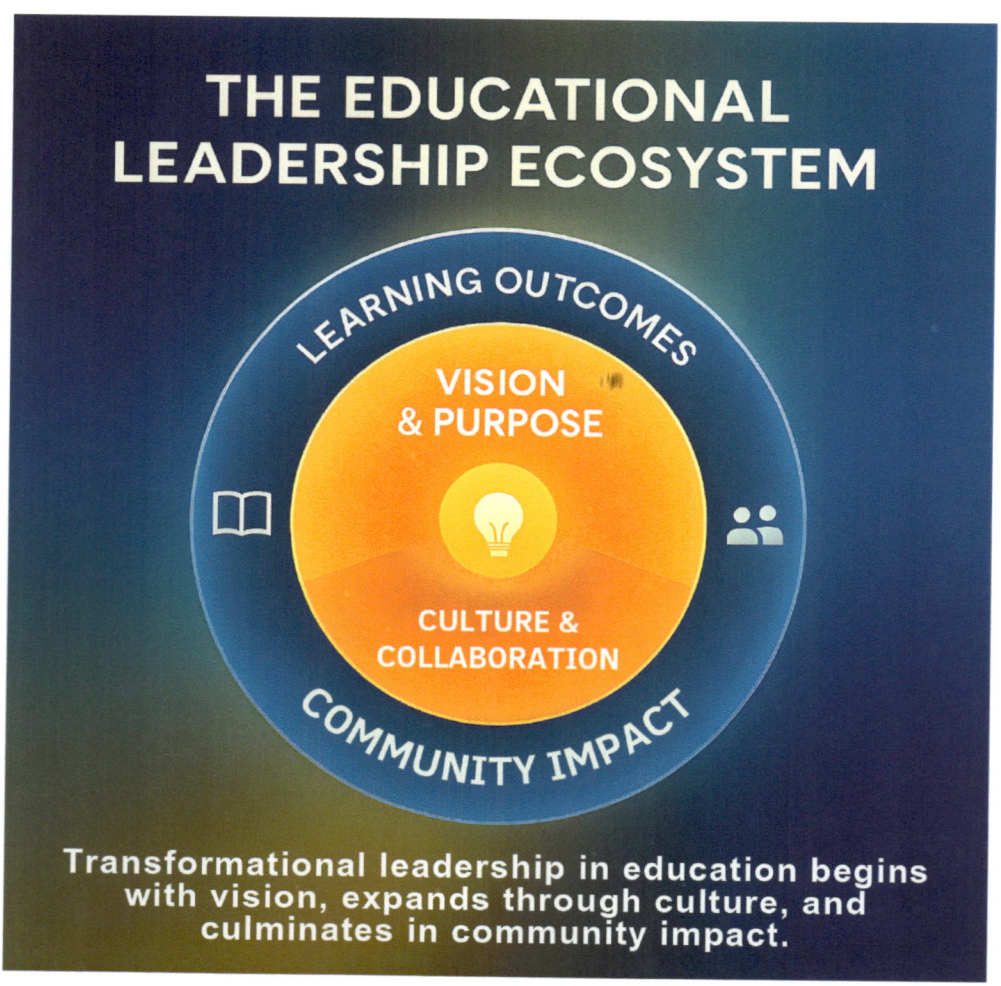

Coaching Strategies for Educational Leaders

Transformational coaching for educational leaders emphasizes several key areas:

- **Vision and Purpose**: Helping leaders articulate a clear, compelling educational mission that inspires both staff and students.

- **Emotional Intelligence**: Developing the self-awareness and empathy needed to build trust, resolve conflict, and foster belonging within diverse school communities.

- **Strengths-Based Leadership**: Encouraging leaders to identify and amplify the unique strengths of staff and faculty rather than focusing only on deficits.

- **Communication and Collaboration**: Building skills for effective dialogue with teachers, parents, boards, and community stakeholders.

These strategies move beyond theory by providing leaders with practical tools for engaging teams, shaping policy, and creating environments where learning thrives.

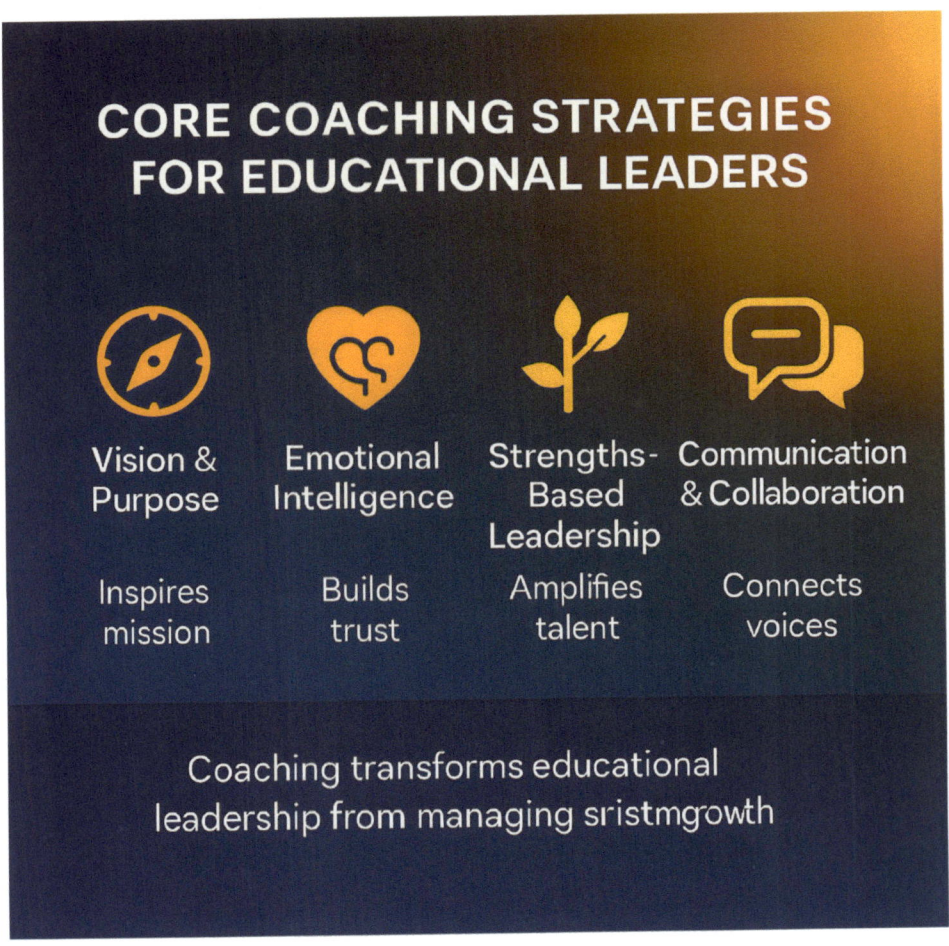

CORE COACHING STRATEGIES FOR EDUCATIONAL LEADERS

Vision & Purpose — Inspires mission

Emotional Intelligence — Builds trust

Strengths-Based Leadership — Amplifies talent

Communication & Collaboration — Connects voices

Coaching transforms educational leadership from managing sristmgrowth

Transforming Educational Institutions through Leadership

Educational institutions face persistent challenges: adapting to new technologies, addressing inequities, managing resource constraints, and preparing students for uncertain futures. Transformational leadership coaching prepares leaders to approach these challenges with creativity, courage, and collaboration.

For example, a principal guided by transformational coaching may focus on cultivating teacher leadership, giving educators a voice in decision-making. A university administrator might use coaching to foster inclusion across a diverse student body. In both cases, the emphasis is the same: aligning vision with practice and empowering individuals to drive meaningful change.

When educational leaders model transformational leadership, they create ripple effects. Students learn not only from curriculum but from the example of leaders who value growth, resilience, and integrity. Coaching reinforces this by holding leaders accountable to both personal development and institutional progress.

Leadership coaching creates ripple effects that amplify learning, equity, and belonging.

Transition to Leadership Development Coaching

Educational leadership illustrates how transformational coaching impacts institutions responsible for shaping the future. The next chapter turns to leadership development coaching, focusing on how organizations can assess needs, design effective programs, and measure results to build leaders who are prepared for tomorrow's challenges.

Modern Case Study

Title: Closing Course Success Gaps at a Community College

Setting: Large urban community college (2024–25).

Challenge: Equity gaps in gateway math/English; faculty fatigue.

Coaching/Approach: Dean led a 'portrait of a learner,' launched a faculty coaching cycle, created a 5-indicator dashboard disaggregated by modality/student group, and held student voice forums.

Results: Gateway pass rates +8 points overall; equity gap narrowed 4 points; DFW in online −6 points.

What to Steal: Pair faculty coaching with disaggregated data and student voice.

Conclusion

Instructional excellence scales when data, coaching, and student voice are integrated. Leaders who focus on a few vital indicators and supportive feedback loops see durable gains in learning and belonging.

Next Steps

- Define a 'portrait of a learner' for two gateway courses.
- Stand up a simple 5-indicator dashboard, disaggregated by course & modality.
- Run a 6-week faculty coaching cycle (observe → feedback → practice).
- Establish a student advisory forum with quarterly themes.
- Publish a 'what we changed' digest each term.

Worksheet

Portrait of a Learner
Capabilities, supports, and assessment signals for success.

_____

_____

_____

_____

_____

Coaching Cycle Planner
Instructor | Focus | Observe date | Feedback date | Practice plan

_____

_____

_____

_____

_____

Course Success Dashboard
Indicators, definitions, targets, owners.

_____

_____

_____

_____

Quick Checklist
☐ I scheduled the key cadences in my calendar.
☐ I identified owners and simple metrics for each action.
☐ I communicated the 'why' and expected outcomes to my team.
☐ I set a 30/60/90 review to assess progress and adjust.

Living on Purpose Prompt: How can staying connected to your purpose strengthen the learning culture within your school or institution?

LIVING ON PURPOSE PROMPT: How can staying connected to your purpose strengthen the learning culture within your school or institution?

Chapter 8 Worksheet

PORTRAIT OF A LEARNER

A learner's portrait reflects both potential and the ecosystem that enables it.

CAPABILITIES
What knowledge, skills, and mindsets define success?

SUPPORTS
What resources or environments enable those skills to grow?

ASSIGNMENT SIGNALS
What evidence shows students are learning and thriving?

COACHING CYCLE PLANNER

INSTRUCTOR: ....

FOCUS: ....

OBSERVE DATE: .... FEEDBACK DATE: ....

PRACTICE PLAN:

....

....

....

....

....

INSTRUCTOR: ....

FOCUS: ....

OBSERVE DATE: .... FEEDBACK DATE: ....

PRACTICE PLAN:

....

....

....

....

....

COACHING CYCLE PLANNER

INSTRUCTOR: ....

FOCUS: ....

OBSERVE DATE: .... FEEDBACK DATE: ....

PRACTICE PLAN:

....

....

....

....

....

INSTRUCTOR: ....

FOCUS: ....

OBSERVE DATE: .... FEEDBACK DATE: ....

PRACTICE PLAN:

....

....

....

....

....

Quick Checklist

◯	I scheduled the key cadences in my calendar.
◯	I identified owners and simple metrics for each action.
◯	I communicated the 'why' and expected outcomes to my team.
◯	I set a 30/60/90 review to assess progress and adjust.

LIVING ON PURPOSE PROMPT

How can staying connected to your purpose strengthen the learning culture within your school or institution?

Assessing Leadership Development Needs

Effective leadership development begins with understanding where leaders are now and where they need to grow. Transformational leadership coaching provides tools to identify these needs through reflection, feedback, and structured assessment.

Assessments may include 360-degree feedback, personality or leadership style inventories, and interviews with key stakeholders. These tools help leaders see their strengths clearly, uncover blind spots, and prioritize growth areas. More importantly, they set the stage for personalized coaching plans that align individual development with organizational strategy.

Coaching also emphasizes self-assessment, encouraging leaders to reflect on their values, motivations, and decision-making tendencies. By combining external feedback with internal reflection, leaders gain a balanced picture of their capabilities and opportunities for growth.

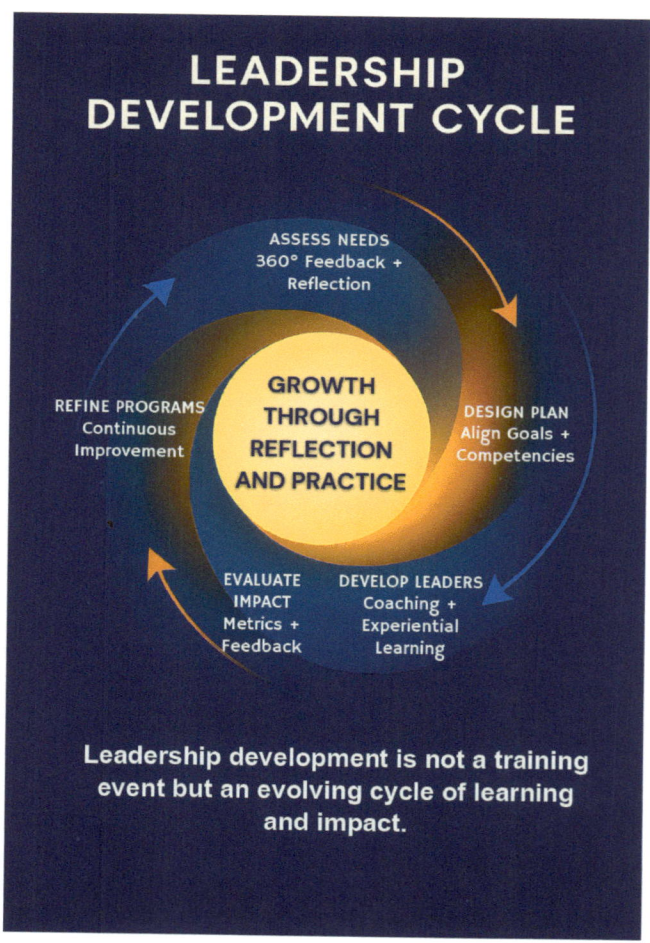

Designing and Implementing Leadership Development Programs

Leadership development is most effective when it is intentional and aligned with organizational goals. Transformational coaching supports program design by focusing on principles that build leaders who inspire, innovate, and empower others.

Key elements of effective programs include:

- **Clear Objectives**: Defining what skills and outcomes the program is designed to achieve.

- **Integration with Strategy**: Ensuring development efforts align with the organization's mission and long-term goals.

- **Experiential Learning**: Using simulations, case studies, and projects that allow leaders to practice in real-world contexts.

- **Mentorship and Coaching**: Pairing leaders with mentors or coaches who provide ongoing guidance, accountability, and support.

- **Diversity and Inclusion**: Designing programs that prepare leaders to lead across cultures, generations, and perspectives.

By grounding these elements in transformational principles—vision, communication, empathy, and innovation—programs build leaders capable of shaping positive organizational culture and achieving lasting results.

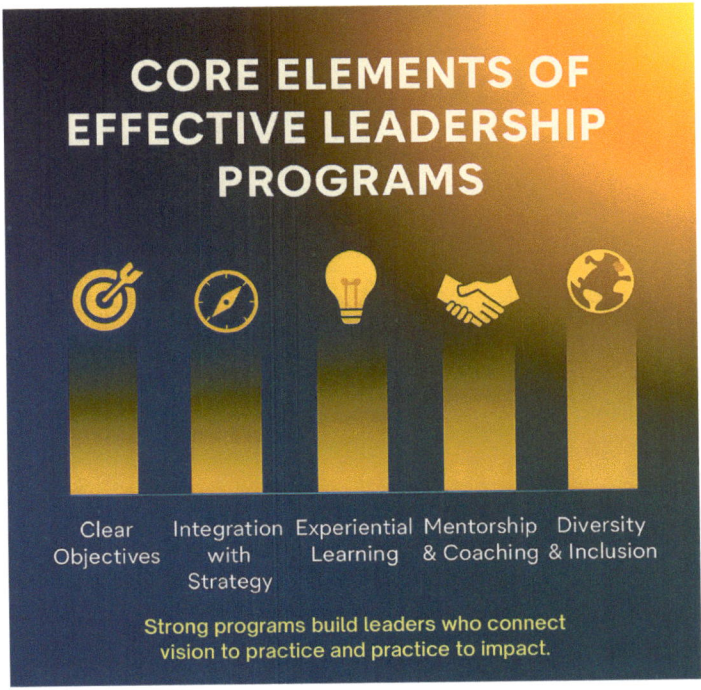

CORE ELEMENTS OF EFFECTIVE LEADERSHIP PROGRAMS

Clear Objectives | Integration with Strategy | Experiential Learning | Mentorship & Coaching | Diversity & Inclusion

Strong programs build leaders who connect vision to practice and practice to impact.

Evaluating the Impact of Leadership Development Initiatives

Assessment does not end when a program is launched. Transformational leadership coaching emphasizes accountability by measuring outcomes and impact. This ensures programs do more than transfer knowledge; they create lasting change.

Evaluation can include surveys, performance metrics, retention data, and follow-up interviews with participants and their teams. Success is measured not only by individual growth but also by organizational outcomes: stronger collaboration, higher engagement, and improved innovation.

Regular evaluation also supports continuous improvement. Leaders and organizations learn which approaches are most effective and refine programs accordingly. This creates a cycle of learning and growth that strengthens leadership capacity across the organization.

Transition to the Future of Transformational Leadership

Leadership development coaching highlights how organizations can intentionally prepare leaders for success. The final chapter turns to the future, exploring how transformational leadership adapts to emerging trends, rapid change, and the demands of a global and interconnected world.

Modern Case Study

Title: Building a Leader Pipeline in a Regional Hospital System

Setting: Four-hospital system with thin bench (2024).

Challenge: 37% of manager roles at risk within 24 months; overreliance on external hires.

Coaching/Approach: Defined competency matrix by level; blended program (workshops + stretch projects + coaching); mentors assigned; evaluation via Kirkpatrick Levels 1–4.

Results: Internal fill rate rose from 28% to 62% in 18 months; time-to-productivity −25%; throughput +7% on units led by alumni.

What to Steal: Tie development to real stretch work and measure behavior change.

Conclusion

Leadership pipelines thrive when learning is job-embedded and measured. Competencies guide focus, stretch work drives growth, and mentoring plus coaching sustain momentum. Evaluate outcomes, not just attendance.

Next Steps

- Draft a 3-tier competency model aligned to strategy.
- Pair each participant with a 90-day stretch project and a mentor.
- Schedule monthly group coaching and quarterly stakeholder reviews.
- Define success using Kirkpatrick Levels 1–4 (reaction → results).
- Publish internal fill-rate and time-to-productivity each quarter.

Worksheet

Level	Core Competencies	Evidence / Behaviors	Development Actions
Emerging Leader			
Mid-Level Leader			
Senior Leader			

Quick Checklist

☐ I scheduled the key cadences in my calendar.
☐ I identified owners and simple metrics for each action.
☐ I communicated the 'why' and expected outcomes to my team.
☐ I set a 30/60/90 review to assess progress and adjust.

Living on Purpose Prompt: How can helping others grow in purpose deepen your own sense of fulfillment as a leader?

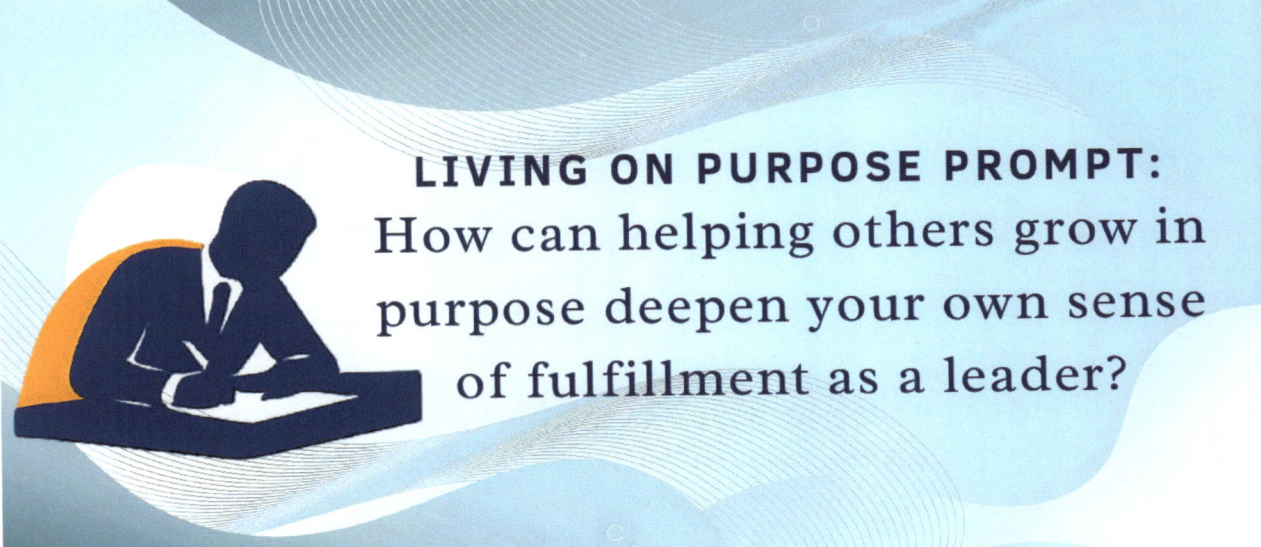

LIVING ON PURPOSE PROMPT: How can helping others grow in purpose deepen your own sense of fulfillment as a leader?

Chapter 9 Worksheet

LEADERSHIP COMPETENCY WORKSHEET

Emerging Leader	Core Compentencies	Development Actions
Mid-Level Leader		
Senior Leader		

**Identify competencies, observe behaviors, and commit
to actions that advance leadership maturity.**

Quick Checklist

◯	I scheduled the key cadences in my calendar.
◯	I identified owners and simple metrics for each action.
◯	I communicated the 'why' and expected outcomes to my team.
◯	I set a 30/60/90 review to assess progress and adjust.

LIVING ON PURPOSE PROMPT

How can helping others grow in purpose deepen your own sense of fulfillment as a leader?

Embracing Change and Innovation in Leadership Coaching

The world of leadership is changing faster than ever. Globalization, digital transformation, and shifting social expectations demand leaders who can adapt quickly and guide others through uncertainty. In this environment, transformational leadership remains relevant not as a static model but as a flexible framework that evolves with new challenges.

Transformational leadership coaching prepares leaders to embrace change with confidence. By fostering a growth mindset, coaching encourages leaders to see disruption not as a threat but as an opportunity for innovation. Leaders who can reframe challenges, inspire creative problem-solving, and communicate a compelling vision will thrive in times of rapid change.

Innovation also requires courage. Transformational leaders model curiosity, encourage experimentation, and create safe spaces for teams to test new ideas. Coaching supports this by equipping leaders with tools for managing risk, learning from failure, and celebrating progress, even when the path forward is uncertain.

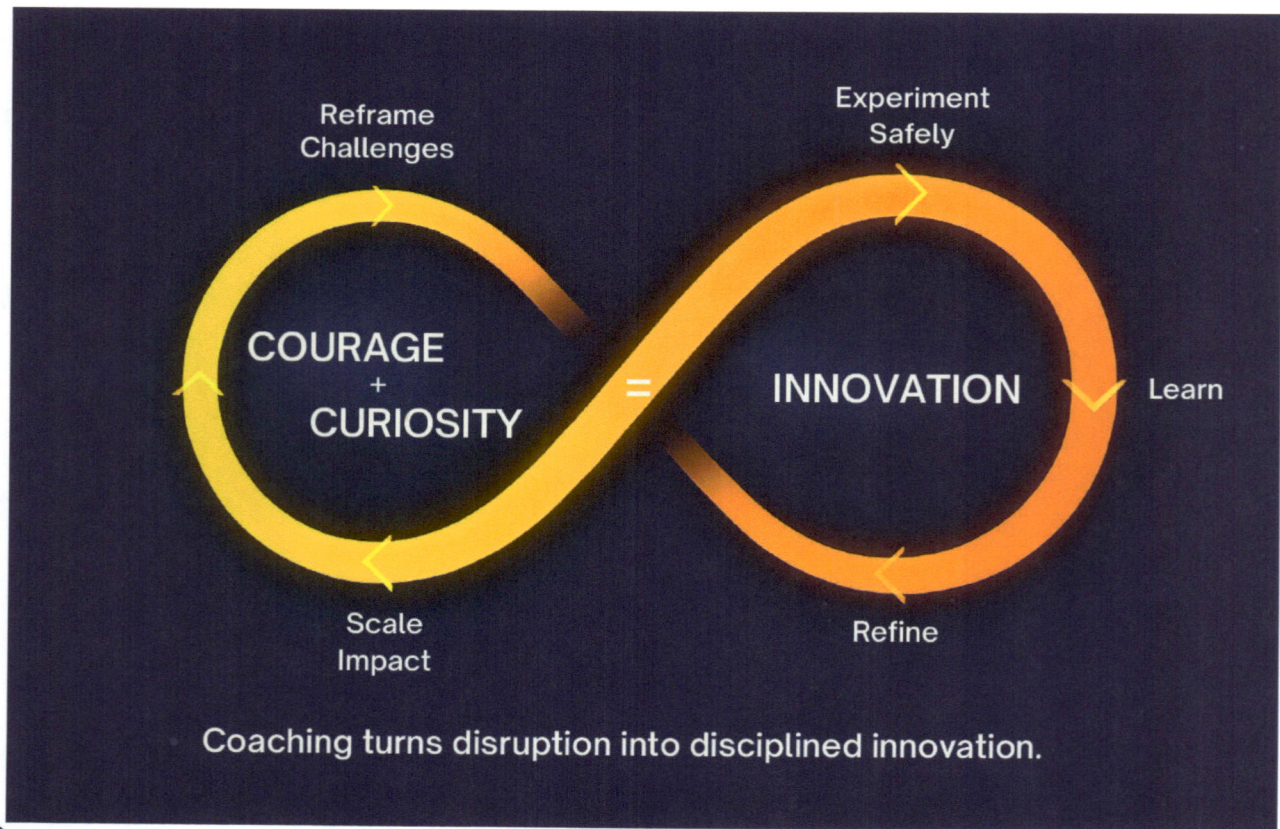

Coaching turns disruption into disciplined innovation.

Adapting to Emerging Trends in Leadership

Several key trends are reshaping the leadership landscape:

- **Technology and AI**: Leaders must balance efficiency with ethics, using tools that enhance decision-making while safeguarding human values.

- **Remote and Hybrid Work**: Flexibility has become essential. Leaders must build trust, sustain culture, and communicate effectively across distance.

- **Generational Shifts**: As Gen Z enters the workforce, expectations for inclusivity, transparency, and purpose-driven leadership continue to rise.

- **Global Challenges**: Issues such as climate change, social justice, and economic instability require leaders to think beyond profit and embrace broader responsibility.

Transformational coaching equips leaders to meet these trends with adaptability. By emphasizing empathy, inclusivity, and vision, coaching ensures leaders remain grounded in human connection even as they navigate technological and cultural change.

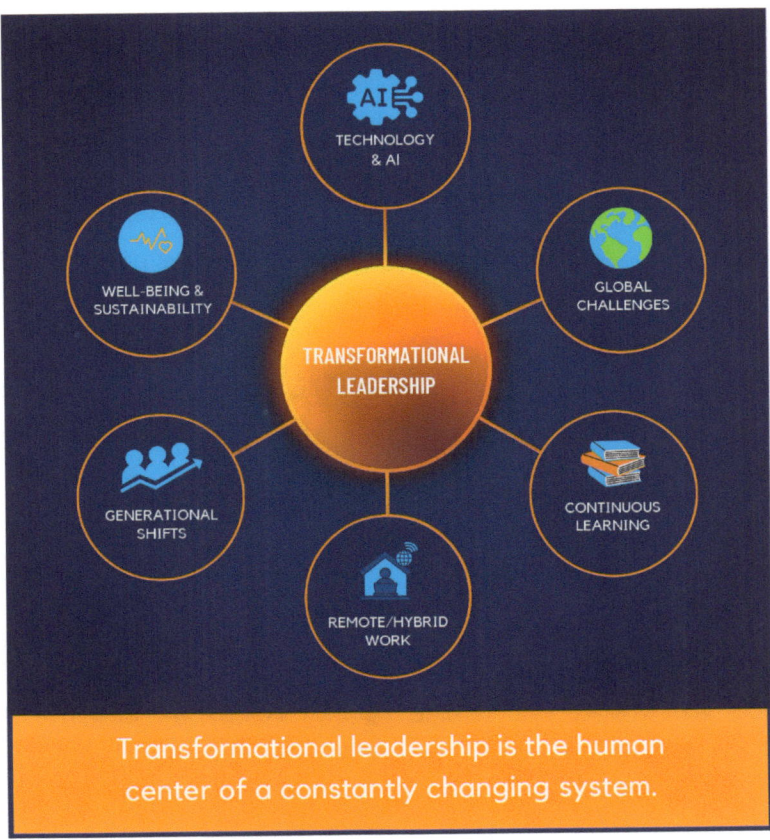

Sustaining Transformational Leadership in the Long Run

Trends may shift, but the need for leaders who inspire, empower, and innovate will endure. Sustaining transformational leadership requires continuous reflection and development. Coaching fosters this sustainability by reinforcing habits of learning, accountability, and resilience.

Leaders who commit to ongoing growth not only strengthen their own capacity but also build organizations that can weather disruption and remain purpose-driven. Over time, this creates a ripple effect: teams become more engaged, cultures become more inclusive, and organizations deliver greater impact.

Transformational leadership is not a passing theory. It is a living approach that adapts to context and equips leaders to meet the future with vision, courage, and integrity.

Transition to Conclusion

The future of leadership highlights why transformational coaching matters today more than ever. It equips leaders to embrace change, adapt to trends, and sustain growth in a world that will only grow more complex. The conclusion brings these themes together, offering encouragement and guidance for leaders committed to unleashing their full potential and leaving a lasting legacy.

Modern Case Study

Title: Ethical AI + Service Excellence in City Government

Setting: Mid-sized city launching AI-assisted 311 triage (2025).

Challenge: Backlogs, resident frustration, union concerns about tech displacement.

Coaching/Approach: Scenario planning, AI guardrails (privacy, bias checks, human-in-loop), 90-day sprint with labor at the table, and weekly communication.

Results: Median response time −35%; first-contact resolution +22%; resident trust +11 points; no net job loss—roles reskilled.

What to Steal: Combine tech experimentation with visible ethics and workforce commitments.

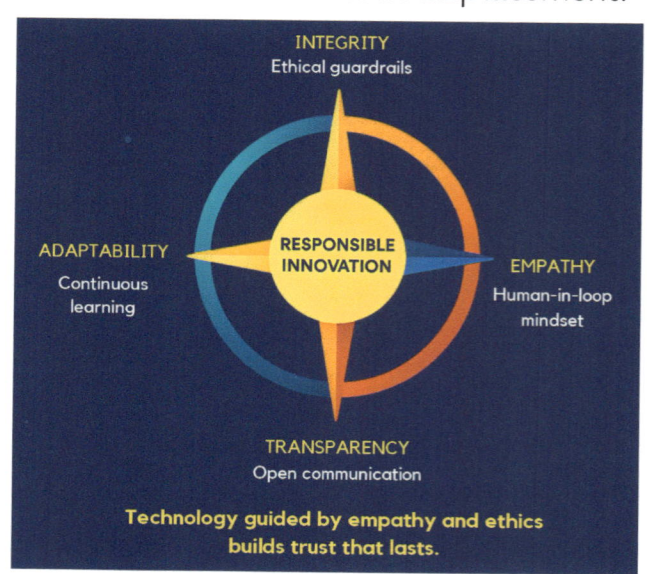

Conclusion

The future rewards leaders who pair innovation with integrity. Scenario thinking, ethical guardrails, and transparent workforce plans turn disruption into trust and better service. Transformational leadership remains human at its core.

Next Steps

- Run a trends & scenarios workshop; identify 3 no-regret moves.
- Publish AI/tech guardrails (privacy, bias, human accountability).
- Launch a 90-day experimentation sprint with 1–2 resident-facing metrics.
- Co-design reskilling pathways with labor or staff councils.
- Tell the change story weekly: what we tried, learned, and changed.

Worksheet

Trend Radar
List 6 trends; rank impact/uncertainty; notes.

_____

_____

_____

Risk–Benefit Canvas (for a tech idea)
Benefits | Risks | Guardrails | Pilot scope | Metrics

_____

_____

_____

Change Story Template
Why now | What changes | What stays | How we'll protect people | How we'll measure

_____

_____

_____

Quick Checklist
- ☐ I scheduled the key cadences in my calendar.
- ☐ I identified owners and simple metrics for each action.
- ☐ I communicated the 'why' and expected outcomes to my team.
- ☐ I set a 30/60/90 review to assess progress and adjust.

Living on Purpose Prompt: What daily practice will keep you aligned with purpose as you navigate the changing world of leadership?

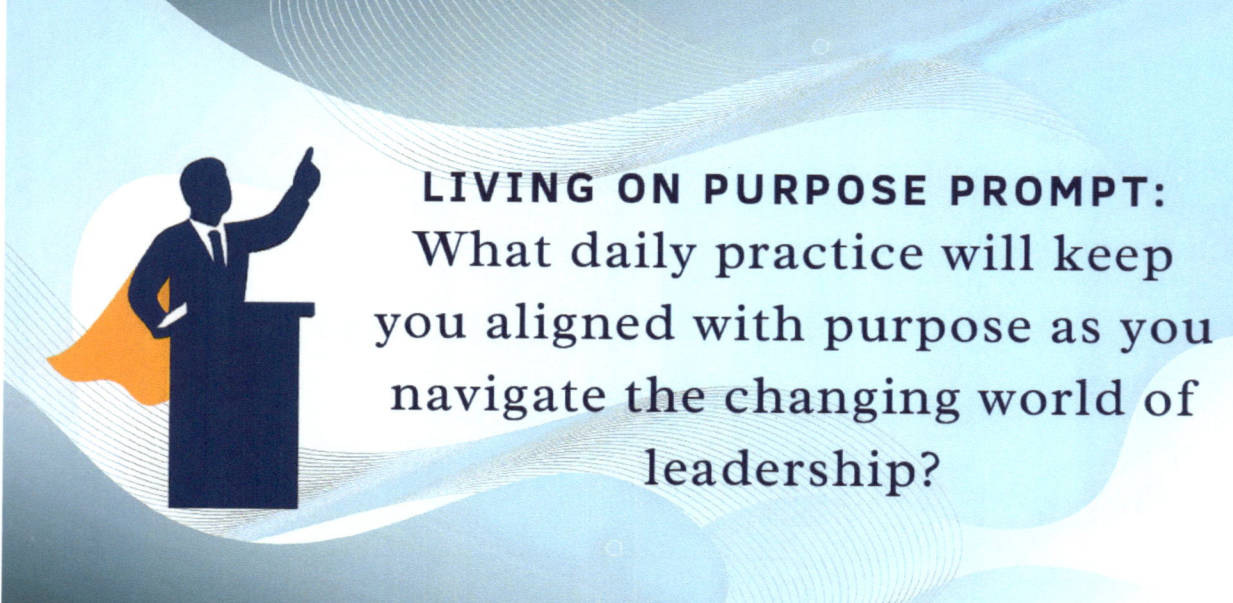

Chapter 10 Worksheet

TREND RADAR

TREND	IMPACT (1-5)	UNCERTAINTY (1-5)	NOTES/IMPLICATIONS

Anticipate what's ahead—impact shows importance, uncertainty reveals opportunity.

RISK BENEFIT CANVAS

BENEFITS	RISKS	GUARDRAILS	PILOT SCOPE	METRICS

Balance innovation with integrity — evaluate ideas through opportunity, risk, and accountability.

CHANGE STORY TEMPLATE

Change stories connect purpose to people — they show not just what shifts,
but how we care while we evolve.

WHY NOW:

....

....

....

WHAT CHANGES:

....

....

....

WHAT STAYS:

....

....

....

HOW WE'LL PROTECT PEOPLE:

....

....

....

HOW WE'LL MEASURE:

....

....

....

CHANGE STORY TEMPLATE

Change stories connect purpose to people — they show not just what shifts,
but how we care while we evolve.

WHY NOW:

....

....

....

WHAT CHANGES:

....

....

....

WHAT STAYS:

....

....

....

HOW WE'LL PROTECT PEOPLE:

....

....

....

HOW WE'LL MEASURE:

....

....

....

Quick Checklist

◯	I scheduled the key cadences in my calendar.
◯	I identified owners and simple metrics for each action.
◯	I communicated the 'why' and expected outcomes to my team.
◯	I set a 30/60/90 review to assess progress and adjust.

LIVING ON PURPOSE PROMPT

Living on Purpose Prompt: What daily practice will keep you aligned with purpose as you navigate the changing world of leadership?

Conclusion: Unleashing Your Full Potential as a Transformational Leader

Recap of Key Concepts and Strategies

Throughout this guide, we have explored how transformational leadership coaching equips leaders to unlock their potential and elevate those around them. We began by defining leadership coaching and distinguishing the qualities that make transformational leadership unique. We examined the traits and practices of transformational leaders, the Four I's that guide their actions, and the ways coaching strengthens leadership in executives, teams, women, nonprofits, millennials, and educational institutions.

We also looked at how organizations can assess leadership development needs, design effective programs, and evaluate results. Finally, we explored how transformational leadership adapts to the emerging trends of the future—technology, hybrid work, generational shifts, and global challenges.

The thread connecting every chapter is clear: transformational leadership coaching is not confined to a role, generation, or industry. It is a flexible, human-centered approach that inspires vision, empowers growth, and sustains long-term success.

THE TRANSFORMATIONAL LEADERSHIP JOURNEY

5. LEGACY

4. IMPACT

3. GROWTH

2. VISION

1. SELF-AWARENESS

Transformation begins within and expands outward-until your growth lifts others.

Encouragement for Continued Growth and Development

Becoming a transformational leader is not a single achievement but a lifelong process. Every leader encounters seasons of challenge, uncertainty, and change. Coaching provides tools for self-reflection, accountability, and resilience to navigate those moments with confidence.

As you continue your journey, remember that growth begins with self-awareness and extends outward. By investing in your own development, you create the capacity to invest in others. By modeling integrity and empathy, you build cultures where people thrive. By sustaining vision and adaptability, you prepare organizations to flourish in uncertain times.

Leadership is a responsibility, but it is also a privilege—the opportunity to shape lives, organizations, and communities for the better.

Final Thoughts on Transformational Leadership

The measure of a transformational leader is not found in titles or positions but in the impact left on others. Each act of inspiration, each moment of empowerment, and each step of resilience builds a legacy that endures beyond immediate results.

As you apply the principles of transformational leadership coaching, you will strengthen not only your own capacity but also the potential of everyone you lead. This is how lasting change begins—leader by leader, conversation by conversation, decision by decision.

The challenge is simple: embrace growth, invest in others, and lead with vision and integrity. In doing so, you will unleash your full potential as a transformational leader and leave a legacy of positive impact that extends well beyond your leadership tenure.

Transformation becomes real through practice. The following section, *The 28-Day Freedom Plan*, is designed to help you turn these principles into daily habits that bring focus, energy, and joy back to your leadership journey."

The 28-Day Freedom Plan: Turning Transformational Habits into a Purpose-Driven Life

Overview: Building a Life That Works for You

Transformation doesn't end when you close this book. It begins when you consistently practice what you've learned.

The 28-Day Freedom Plan is designed to help you do exactly that—to turn awareness into rhythm, and rhythm into freedom.

Most people don't lack motivation; they lack structure. This plan provides a framework that helps you translate intention into action without feeling overwhelmed. The next four weeks will help you realign your habits with your purpose so that progress feels sustainable, not stressful.

The concept is simple: **it takes consistent practice to turn a habit into a lifestyle.** In twenty-eight days, you'll build a foundation that helps you work smarter, rest intentionally, and live with clarity.

The Rhythm of Freedom: Preparation and Execution

Each week, you'll organize your schedule into three types of days:

1. **Preparation Days** – These are your planning and setup days. You focus on organization, visioning, and getting ready for what's ahead. Preparation builds momentum and confidence.

   - *Examples:* Setting priorities, reviewing goals, cleaning your workspace, scheduling meetings, or prepping meals.

2. **Execution Days** – These are your focused action days. You commit to working with intention on the goals or projects you've prepared for—without distraction or multitasking.

   - *Examples:* Completing reports, delivering presentations, making client calls, writing, teaching, or mentoring.

3. **Freedom Days** – These are your rest, renewal, and reflection days. You give yourself permission to recharge without guilt. Freedom Days are not a reward; they are a requirement for longevity and joy.

   - *Examples:* Reading for pleasure, exercising, connecting with loved ones, prayer, travel, or simply doing nothing at all.

The balance of these days keeps you aligned and energized. You'll typically have **two to three Preparation Days**, **two to three Execution Days**, and **two Freedom Days** each week. The key is that you honor the purpose of the day you're in.

When you prepare, prepare fully.

When you execute, execute boldly.

When you rest, rest completely.

The Power of Focused Consistency

Consistency creates confidence. By repeating this rhythm for 28 days, you'll train your mind and body to operate with purpose and peace. This plan will help you:

- Eliminate procrastination and decision fatigue.

- Build clarity around your priorities.

- Reconnect with your sense of purpose and joy.

- Accomplish more in less time, with less stress.

Remember: you are not just managing your time—you are designing your life.

WEEKLY FREEDOM SCHEDULE

Mon	Tues	Wed	Thurs	Fri	Sat	Sun

Plan your rhythm. Protect your peace.

How to Use This Plan

- **Weekly Freedom Schedule:** Use the worksheet provided to color-code your Prep, Exec, and Freedom Days.

- **Daily Check-In:** Write your morning intention and close the day with a short reflection.

- **Progress Tracker:** Mark your 28 days of commitment and celebrate your wins along the way.

- **Debrief:** At the end of the plan, review what improved most in your focus, energy, or joy—and decide which habits to keep as part of your permanent rhythm.

By the end of 28 days, you will have done more than complete a challenge—you will have created a pattern of living and leading on purpose.

Reflection Prompt:

What would freedom look like for you in this season of your life—and what habits are standing in the way?

Reflection Prompt:

What would freedom look like for you in this season of your life—and what habits are standing in the way?

_____

_____

_____

Using Your Freedom Schedule Worksheet

Use this worksheet to design your weekly rhythm with intention. Begin by color-coding each day of the week: Blue for Preparation, Orange for Execution, and Yellow for Freedom. In each column, write your Focus, Key Tasks, and Notes to keep priorities clear. The goal isn't to fill every moment, but to bring structure to your energy and balance to your time. When you prepare, prepare fully. When you execute, execute boldly. When you rest, rest completely.

Review your schedule weekly and adjust as needed to maintain alignment between your purpose and your pace.

Quick Checklist

◯	I scheduled the key cadences in my calendar.
◯	I identified owners and simple metrics for each action.
◯	I communicated the 'why' and expected outcomes to my team.
◯	I set a 30/60/90 review to assess progress and adjust.

LIVING ON PURPOSE PROMPT

Living on Purpose Prompt: What daily practice will keep you aligned with purpose as you navigate the changing world of leadership?

Weekly Freedom Schedule

■ PREPARATION ■ EXECUTION ■ FREEDOM

	FOCUS	KEY TASKS	NOTES
MONDAY			
TUESDAY			
WEDNESDAY			
THURSDAY			
FRIDAY			
SATURDAY			
SUNDAY			

Weekly Freedom Schedule

■ PREPARATION   ■ EXECUTION   ■ FREEDOM

	FOCUS	KEY TASKS	NOTES
MONDAY			
TUESDAY			
WEDNESDAY			
THURSDAY			
FRIDAY			
SATURDAY			
SUNDAY			

Weekly Freedom Schedule

■ PREPARATION   ■ EXECUTION   ■ FREEDOM

	FOCUS	KEY TASKS	NOTES
MONDAY			
TUESDAY			
WEDNESDAY			
THURSDAY			
FRIDAY			
SATURDAY			
SUNDAY			

Weekly Freedom Schedule

🟦 PREPARATION   🟧 EXECUTION   🟨 FREEDOM

	FOCUS	KEY TASKS	NOTES
MONDAY			
TUESDAY			
WEDNESDAY			
THURSDAY			
FRIDAY			
SATURDAY			
SUNDAY			

From Worksheets to Rhythm: Starting Your Freedom Journal
You don't need 28 separate pages to stay consistent — just one intentional rhythm.
Use the **Daily Check-In Sheet** as a guide to start or continue your personal journal.
Each day, take 5 minutes in the morning and 5 minutes in the evening to pause, write, and reflect.
Whether you use a notebook, digital app, or voice memo, the key is consistency — not perfection.

Journal Rhythm:

Morning — Write your *focus* and *intentions.*

Evening — Reflect on *progress* and *gratitude.*

You're not just logging tasks; you're capturing transformation in real time.

Daily Check-In Sheet

☀ MORNING FOCUS

What is my focus today?

What habit or mindset will support that focus?

What could distract me, and how will I stay centered?

How do I want to feel at the end of today?

🌙 EVENING REFLECTION

What gave me energy or joy today?

What challenged me, and what did I learn from it?

What progress did I make toward my goals?

What's one thing I'll carry into tomorrow?

Using Your 28-Day Progress Tracker

This tracker helps you see your consistency at a glance. Each box represents one day of your 28-day journey. Check it off, color it in, or mark it with a symbol that reflects how you showed up that day. Celebrate progress, not perfection — the goal is rhythm, not rigidity. At the end of each week, use the **Milestone Notes** section to record key insights, shifts in mindset, or small wins that fueled your motivation.

28-Day Progress Tracker

Each box represents one day of your 28-day journey.
Celebrate progress, not perfection.

1	2	3	4	5	6	7

Milestone Notes

_____

_____

_____

_____

_____

8	9	10	11	12	13	14

Milestone Notes

_____

_____

_____

_____

_____

15	16	17	18	19	20	21

Milestone Notes

_____

_____

_____

_____

_____

22	23	24	25	26	27	28

Milestone Notes

_____

_____

_____

_____

_____

 ***Transformation doesn't happen in a day
...it happens day by day.***

From Practice to Purpose: The 28-Day Reflection

You've now completed the 28-Day Freedom Plan — a journey of intention, structure, and self-discovery. The habits you've practiced over the past four weeks are more than checkboxes; they're building blocks for a lifestyle grounded in purpose. Before moving forward, take a moment to pause and reflect. This debrief is your opportunity to celebrate growth, acknowledge lessons, and identify which rhythms will carry you into the next chapter of your leadership and life.

Transformation is not a finish line—it's a rhythm. What you've built over these past 28 days is a foundation for continued clarity, courage, and consistency. Revisit this process whenever life feels cluttered or direction feels unclear. Each new season offers another opportunity to realign your habits with your purpose. Keep leading yourself with intention, and freedom will follow.

28-Day Debrief Worksheet
Looking Back to Move Forward

Reflect on your growth over the past four weeks. Use this page to celebrate wins, note insights, and plan your next steps.

What improved most in my energy, focus, or joy?

Which habits felt most natural to sustain?

What challenges or distractions did I overcome?

What new opportunities or possibilities do you see as a result of this process?

What will I do differently in the next 28 days to stay aligned with my purpose?

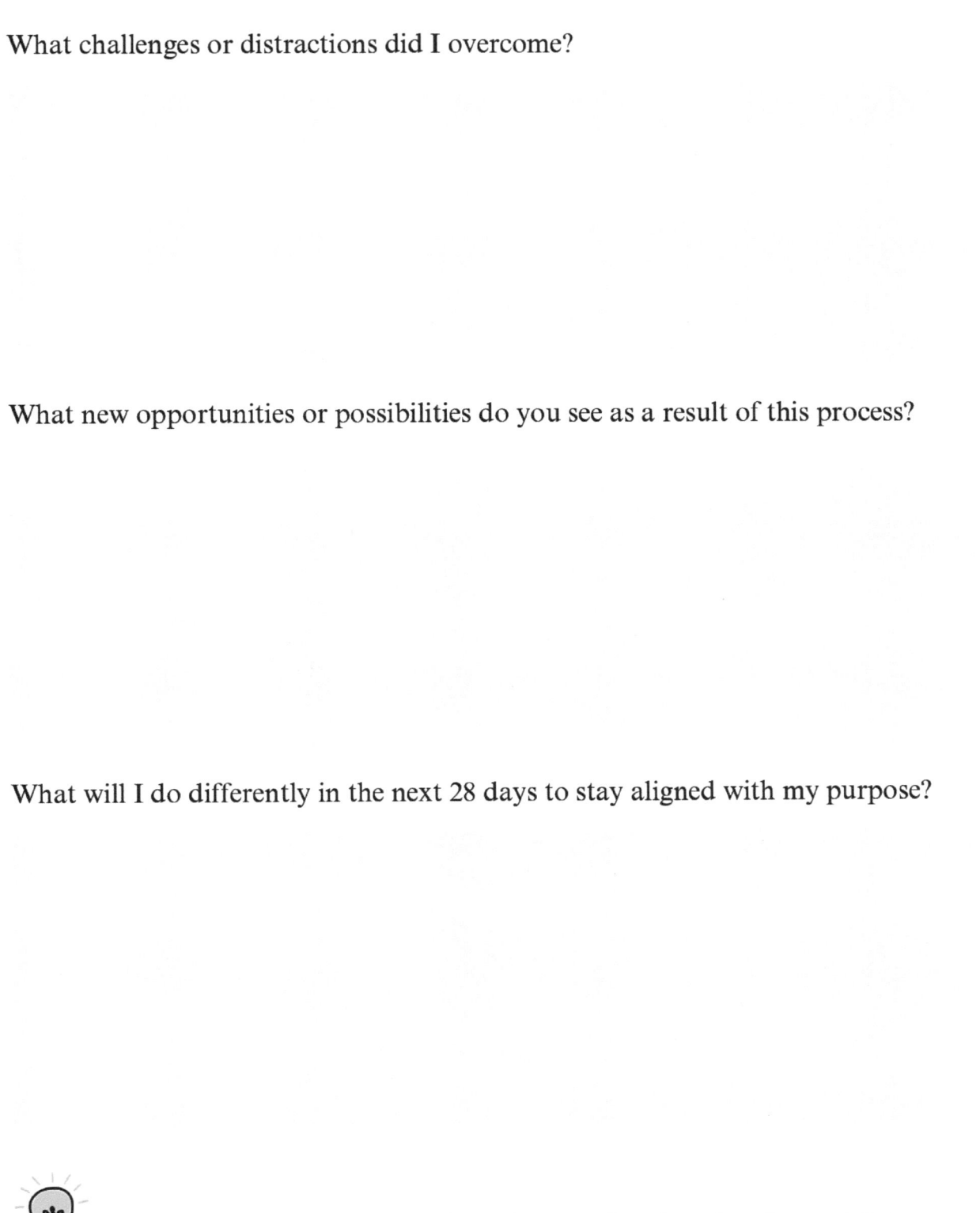 **Remember: Freedom isn't found in perfection, but in consistency....**

Also available:

Transformational Leadership Workbook: Your Coaching Companion to Unleashing Your Full Potential

Build on what you've learned with guided exercises, reflection prompts, and tools to help you live and lead on purpose.

Acknowledgments

I extend my deepest gratitude to Dr. Harvey Fields, Dean of the College of STEM at Harris-Stowe State University. Harvey's thoughtful edits, insightful suggestions, and meticulous attention to formatting strengthened this book at every stage. His steady encouragement—and his willingness to challenge ideas in the spirit of clarity and rigor—made the manuscript sharper, more accessible, and truer to its purpose. I am grateful for his time, expertise, and friendship.

Jonathan K. Jefferson, D.Mgmt.

President, Roxbury Community College

Dr. Jonathan K. Jefferson is a mission-driven higher education leader and transformation strategist who serves as President of Roxbury Community College (RCC). Since assuming the presidency in 2024, he has launched **Roxbury 2030**, a long-term institutional strategy positioning RCC as a nationally recognized, equity-driven urban community college. In his first year, Dr. Jefferson closed a **$3.4M budget deficit**, strengthened governance by establishing a permanent Executive Operations Team and a Vice President for Enterprise Transformation, and advanced core institutional plans, including the five-year Strategic Plan, Strategic Enrollment Plan, Academic Portfolio Review, and Strategic Marketing & Communications Plan.

Under his leadership, RCC has modernized technology and student services through a **22-project IT portfolio**—migrating to Canvas LMS, implementing Slate CRM, optimizing Jenzabar, and opening two new computer labs that provide more than **300 laptops and desktops** for on-demand access. He led operational reforms and community re-engagement at the Reggie Lewis Track & Athletic Center, secured the **largest-ever state appropriation** for the facility, and helped anchor a **$1.3M gift** from the Boston Athletic Association. In development, he expanded staff capacity and helped secure **$1.8M in private funding** and **$1.7M in government grants**, while elevating RCC's visibility through data-informed enrollment marketing that generated over **1,500 new student inquiries**.

Prior to RCC, Dr. Jefferson served as **Chief Academic Officer and Provost** at Lesley University (2020–2023) and later as **Special Advisor to the President**. At Lesley, he ensured academic quality and alignment across programs; led inclusive, anti-racist, and culturally sustaining pedagogy initiatives; built proactive advising and field-placement models; and designed first- and second-year experiences centered on diversity and student success. Earlier at Lesley, as **Division Director of Business Management** (2015–2020), he redesigned the B.S. in Business Management, launched a 4+1 MBA, guided the development of 27+ new courses, and led the unit to **ACBSP accreditation in under 24 months**.

Dr. Jefferson's leadership development work spans the **U.S. Coast Guard Academy**, where he served as **Director of the Institute for Leadership** (2010–2014), architecting a comprehensive leader development strategy (LEAD), creating 360-degree feedback instruments, and authoring the **Leader Development Playbook**. He previously served as **Dean** at **Albany State University** (2009–2010) and **Clark Atlanta University** (2004–2007), where he raised significant philanthropic support, modernized academic operations, and built signature programs (financial trading center, collaborative learning spaces, LEAD Week, consulting clinics) that strengthened student success and external partnerships.

Before academia, Dr. Jefferson built a distinguished career in management consulting and industry with senior roles at **A.T. Kearney** (Vice President & Officer), **CSC Consulting** (Partner), **BearingPoint** (Director), **Price Waterhouse**(Manager), and corporate appointments at **BellSouth** (Executive Director of Strategic Planning & Corporate Development), **Citibank**, and **AT&T Bell Laboratories**. His consulting portfolio includes operational transformations, enterprise PMOs, portfolio optimization, cost reductions, and digital strategy for Fortune 100 firms and global telecoms, producing hundreds of millions of dollars in identified savings and measurable performance gains.

An active scholar-practitioner, Dr. Jefferson has published on leader development, trust, mentoring, and management in journals such as the **Journal of Leadership Studies** and **Journal of Multidisciplinary Research**, and contributed to **T+D Magazine** ("Leadership Is Everybody's Business"). He has served on accreditation teams (AACSB, ACBSP, SACSCOC, ABHE) and chaired boards, including **W.L. Bonner College**.

Dr. Jefferson holds a **Doctor of Management** (Colorado Technical University), an **M.S. in Organization and Management** (Capella University), an **M.Eng. in Operations Research & Industrial Engineering** (Cornell University), and a **B.S. in Mathematics, with honors** (Morehouse College). He is a **Certified Leadership Challenge Facilitator**, **Certified Six Sigma Green Belt**, **Certified Manager**, **Certified Behavioral Consultant/Analyst**, and completed the **PMP** examination (credential dormant). His professional development includes the **HBCU Executive Leadership Institute** fellowship.

Across higher education, public service, and industry, Dr. Jefferson is known for uniting strategy with execution—advancing equity, strengthening institutional resilience, and developing leaders who deliver meaningful, measurable impact for students and communities.

www.ingramcontent.com/pod-product-compliance
Lightning Source LLC
Chambersburg PA
CBHW041427120626
46547CB00002B/123